Beat the Banks

To John Lu

L.A Convention Expo
2/22/09 $20—

John Lu

Beat the Banks

How to Prosper in the Rising Wave of Bank Foreclosures

Steve Dexter

National Capitol Funding

For further information, please contact:
stevedexter@hotmail.com

Book design by Arbor Books
www.arborbooks.com

Printed in the United States of America

Beat the Banks: How to Prosper in the Rising Wave of Bank Foreclosures
Steve Dexter

1. Title 2. Author 3. Profit and build wealth by buying bank foreclosures

Library of Congress Control Number: 2008939563

ISBN 10: 0-9821928-0-0
ISBN 13: 978-0-9821928-0-1

Table of Contents

INTRODUCTION

Welcome to *the new era*, a new time in the real estate market when the hugest distress is not predominately felt by homeowners in foreclosure. It is the banks, the lenders, hedge funds on Wall Street and the American economy that are in turmoil. *The lenders have the deals.* And more are coming.

Don't believe me? Countrywide Credit, one of the largest lenders in the country, based in Calabasas, CA, would disagree with you. The chart above shows that since January 27, 2007, its REOs in inventory (bank-owned property taken back in foreclosure after the borrower failed to make the required payments) doubled from an amount of slightly over 5,000 to 15,108 properties. Its foreclosed inventory has exploded by 10,108 more houses, an increase of 202%. They have got to liquidate, and, as we will see, this is just the beginning.

Are Californians immune from this rising wave? Is the United States' most populous region, with all its healthy demographics, huge foreign immigration, and the most millionaires and billionaires in the galaxy, immune to this coming trend? Hardly.

Keep reading.

It is worse in California, which has over 20% of Countrywide's REOs. Its website now shows an REO inventory numbering 4,370, an increase of 420% in just eleven months. As with many lenders, its problems are likely just starting. Last year, Countrywide was the volume leader in funding pay option

ARMs, a kind of loan in which the borrower's payments start at an ultra low rate of around 1%.

Countrywide was so astounded to find that over 75% of its customers were paying only the minimum payment option that it sent a warning letter to them. If you keep making this payment, it advised, you will ***experience a doubling or tripling in your house payment.***

Over nine California properties a day are being added to Countrywide's foreclosed inventory, and the pace is accelerating.

Countrywide is not alone. Take a look at the next chart, which shows us the billions of dollars of all kinds of adjustable rate loans due to reset.

The pay option ARMs are in tan and all the subprime loans are in green. What this chart is telling us is that the option ARM loans will be hitting their peak reset fifty-five months out from January 2007 or June 2011. The subprime loans adjusting will hit their high in November 2008.

A crest in the wave of loan resets starts in late 2007 and continues until early 2012. Pretty revealing, huh?

More than one million American homes are expected to enter foreclosure this year, and some estimates say that number is closer to two million. The total represents about 2.3%-4.3% of the nation's forty-four million home loans, according to Freddie Mac, which bases its estimate on data provided by the Mortgage Bankers Association, a Washington-based trade group. Freddie Mac says about 60% of those homes carry subprime mortgages. Subprime mortgages are home loans made to borrowers with shaky credit records. Banks, lenders and industry officials use the word *"**staggering**"* to describe the number of loans whose teaser and fixed rates will expire soon—up to $1.5 trillion in loans this year, according to the Mortgage Bankers Association.

The projected foreclosure rate—higher than during the oil bust of 1987—poses a significant threat to the housing sector, and possibly to the nation's economy, if it spurs consumers to maintain a tight grip on their wallets.

Some people may be scared, particularly those who have one

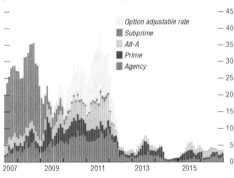

Figure 1.7. Monthly Mortgage Rate Resets
(First reset in billions of U.S. dollars)

Source: Credit Suisse.

Option ARM loans will hit their peak reset in June, 2011. Subprime loan adjustments peaked in Nov., 2008.

of what I call "Frankenstein loans." Too many people who got these loans will be unprepared for the future consequences of what kind of loan choice they made. They:

1. Did not read my first book, *Real Estate Debt Can Make You Rich*;
2. Were ill-informed by loan sharks who did not see fit to explain the good and bad of how these loans work.

The loan industry will suffer from government over-regulation because of the sins of those few greedy criminals.

The future of Frankenstein loan recipients is set in stone because many will not be able to refinance since their interest rates will be higher and their equity is up in smoke.

I say don't be scared, get excited. Never before have we seen real estate downturn fueled by Frankenstein.

CHAPTER 1

Why I Want to Teach You This

All my life I have had a special interest in finance, but you would not know it from the type of degree I got when I graduated from the University of Oklahoma back in 1977. You would think by me obtaining a Bachelor of Science degree in psychology that I did not have much interest in the world of business. As a matter of fact, I discovered early on that psychology was one of the few degrees I could get without taking a bunch of math prerequisites. The world of numbers intimidated me. I stayed far away from it.

Like most newly minted college graduates, I struggled to find my place in the world. Upon graduation, I became a social worker for the Oklahoma Department of Human Services, helping the old, infirm and disabled qualify for state aid. My superiors were unimpressed with me.

I wonder if it had to do with the fact that on my first day on the job, I took a half day off. It was not a good fit.

Mortgage Broker/Lender
Years later, after drifting from job to job, I was tired of being broke. I was wandering aimlessly, looking for where I fit in. Then it hit me: "I know what I'll do! *I am going to get rich in real estate*. A glamorous career in real estate is for me and I'll make a million bucks. Yessirree, I am going to set the world on fire and get rich in real estate and then I'm going to retire and take life easy."

Many people start off thinking that way—that real estate is the easy path to riches. If that is you, I say don't jump the gun and quit your day job. Don't get cocky or underestimate the challenges that will face you. If you decide to buy foreclosed property for a quick re-sell (flip), buy a distressed house to hold in your portfolio for long-term wealth accumulation or become employed in the business of listing property; you will have to dig deep into your well of persistence and determination to make it in the business of real estate. You must be unwavering and diligent.

I Had a Lot to Learn

I ran into problems soon with my first foray into real estate moguldom. Sound familiar?

As a fledgling mortgage broker, I discovered it was not that easy being on straight commission, as most people do who are in the field of real estate. I found out that I was more attuned to being a mortgage lender rather than a real estate agent because I found that the numbers and math I had always feared were much more interesting when they had dollar signs attached to them.

When I got my real estate license in 1990, interest rates were on their way down so I rode the refinance wave. When interest rates decline, borrowers rush to refinance their existing loans to take advantage of the lower rates. Business was good. Then it wasn't.

Interest rates rose again (don't they always?) and my clientele dwindled. People were not refinancing anymore. I strived mightily to find clients and found I did not know much about how to retain clients. I was always looking for new leads and new prospects to fund more deals so I could eat. Does this resonate with any of you real estate salespeople?

It did not help that in the 1990s, Southern California was going through the worst real estate recession since the Great Depression. *Property values went down as much as 40% in some areas.*

I tried everything. I solicited business from banks, started a leads group where we exchanged sales leads, and went to local chamber of commerce meetings. I even walked around neighborhoods putting flyers on doors.

I paid retail for a three-unit building in Huntington Beach. Obviously, with three years as a mortgage broker, I knew everything about real estate. Wrong! Property management was a skill I had not yet acquired. I had trouble keeping all units filled with paying tenants. Knowing how to choose neighborhoods that were not declining was something I had yet to learn. Plus, in 1994, a declining Southern California real estate market pushed down my property value by $50,000. Maintenance expenses ate me up, tenants ran me ragged and I always seemed to have a unit vacant.

Am I Ringing Any Bells out There?

Since I paid retail, I had no buffer. Because I didn't know how to manage property, I had sporadic cash flow and flaky tenants. If you buy REOs priced below market, you have a little wiggle room if you mess up. If you know property management, your tenants pay off your property. I lost that property to foreclosure one and a half years later, as well as $40,000 in expenses and negative cash flow and my original down payment.

So my first experience in REO property was that I produced one. I never want to be on the wrong side of a bank foreclosure again. I want to profit from distressed property, not be the victim of it.

Business Slowly Started to Improve

As my business and income grew, I started setting aside money for investment. Ten to twenty percent of almost every check went directly to a money market fund and a mutual fund. My wife and I bought a house in Laguna Beach, CA.

I think getting married had something to do with me getting serious in the field of real estate. My wife remains my biggest supporter and staunchest ally today. Since she and her family have a long heritage of investing in real estate, I have learned much about the wealth-building value of buying and holding real estate for the long term.

I Started Looking at Foreclosures

So we started buying foreclosed houses from the Veterans Administration with low to no down payments. It was not hard if you did not mind putting up with some of its arcane rules. There were lots of arbitrary deadlines and they were always threatening to give the property to the next buyer if we did not toe the line.

When you buy homes from the Veterans Administration (VA), you are taking over a house repossessed from a defaulting member of the armed services. The VA does not make the actual loan but guarantees the loan, so the bank making the loan takes very little risk. The VA smoothes the way for service people to buy houses using these easy- to-qualify loans. If the homeowner has to suddenly relocate or is abruptly reassigned to another station, the VA takes the house back. Many times the defaulting service member does not even get a foreclosure on his or her credit report.

For investors, most of the repossessed houses that the VA makes available have what is called VA vendee financing. But not with all houses will they give those easy-to-qualify loans.

For awhile it was easy, but soon the VA homes dried up. It always happens when the local real estate market starts to heat up that the pickings of government repossessed homes become slim. If we wanted to keep buying property, we had to do something different.

"I know," I said to my wife. "Let's go knock on doors and buy foreclosures!" Isn't that what all the late-night TV hucksters and seminar gurus say? They said foreclosed-on homeowners would be glad to hand over their house keys to us because they needed our help.

We hit the streets and started knocking on the troubled homeowners' doors. Every Sunday after church we drove all over town to talk to the people we found listed in the foreclosure tracking service's website. We were saints by morning and vultures by afternoon.

What we experienced most weekends were front doors slamming in our faces. We were not very good at it. Some people were nice, but most of them did not want to talk to us when they found out what we were there for. Many lied and said everything was alright and taken care of. But we knew better. We actually had limited success—we sat at about six kitchen tables inside six foreclosed houses, but never got a deal. Either something was materially wrong with the house or we could not negotiate the price we wanted.

After awhile, after my bleary eyes had finished looking at lists after lists of property going through the various stages of foreclosure, I started calling the trustees (who handle the legal process of foreclosed properties) and the beneficiaries (the actual lender). One trustee gave the internal bank phone number of the REO department. Somebody at the bank who I could actually talk to about an actual property? I thought it was hard to find anybody at this big, nameless, faceless bank who had any power.

But, sure enough, when I called, they faxed over a list of foreclosed properties that afternoon. **PAYDIRT!** I remember it like it was yesterday because the next morning after we looked at a couple of those properties, we made an offer that afternoon. It was listed with a Realtor named Norm. He actually helped us on what to say to the REO lady so we were able to get a great price on that property, which was listed for $219,000.

Seven days later, on the day after Christmas, we signed loan documents to close on 1989–era, two- story house for $165,000—a 25% discount. On top of that, the bank gave us a great loan on what is called expedited financing (more about that later). That property is worth a lot more today.

That's my story. Now, let's talk about you.

Late-Night Hucksters Make Foreclosure Investing Sound Easy

Everybody is entranced with buying a foreclosure, as though that is the sure-fire path to wealth. I cannot tell you how many times I have heard that "I have been to this seminar and I am so excited. The speaker said I can buy a house from somebody facing hard times for thirty percent, forty percent (you supply the number) below market value."

There is a growing epidemic of smooth-talking salesman on late-night TV expounding on the benefits of buying property through foreclosure. They have pictures of beautiful houses bought in other areas for twenty cents on the dollar. If you just buy their low-cost system today, in three easy payments you will get rich and attain all those beautiful girls, sporty yachts and big houses. But they never tell you exactly where those houses are (or where the girls are). *Most foreclosure seminars that are big on the lifestyle stuff are dream factories.*

Maybe there is meat in what some of those gurus have to say. Maybe you can buy from people going into foreclosure or perhaps even buy at the fore-closure auction. But before you invest thousands in the unknown, and try to buy pre-foreclosure directly from owners, let me ask you some questions:

1. Can you talk to owners in distress?
2. Do you have the skills necessary to create a win-win purchase from harried homeowners getting ready to lose their houses?
3. Can you negotiate fast enough to lock up the deal before a more experienced foreclosure buyer swoops in?
4. Do you know how to arrange seller financing or at least have a well-moneyed investor/partner to give walking-away money to the homeowner?
5. If you are going to flip it, can you buy the house low enough (30%-40% below market) to make a profit and pay all carrying and sales costs?
6. If you are buying at a foreclosure auction, do you have it all in cash?
7. Since you probably have not been inside the house, are you ready for the property defects that are yet to be discovered?
8. Do you have a lead-generating machine?
9. Are you indefatigable enough to chase every deal in town to create a pipeline of future transactions?

Lots of deals fall out of escrow. When you close a deal, you need to have a system to replace it with another.

I have found the people who make a lot of money buying pre-foreclosures or at foreclosure sales are the most experienced or the most diligent. If you don't have experience or money, youth, energy and a can-do spirit is a good place to start.

The best way to make money in the property investment game is to buy in times of distress from people in distress, or distressed property that needs to be fixed up. Practically every property I have bought has been a distressed sale in one form or another.

CHAPTER 2

Making Money in Real Estate to Increase Your Cash Flow and Wealth for the Rest of Your Life

The REO Market Is Booming Again

When real estate markets began to heat up, fewer properties go through fore-closure because homeowners can sell or refinance if they get into difficulty.

My wife and I went on to buy more property, some more through bank repossessions. Then we had to move on to other buying strategies since the REO market dried up.

We now have a booming REO market. I want you to have the same experience as I did, so that is why I have written this book.

In the process of buying twenty-seven investment properties, I wrote two courses, "The Top 15 Laws of Highly Successful Real Estate Investors" and "How to Get the Absolute Best Loan for Your Home or Investment Properties," which I teach at community colleges. I wrote a top-rated investment book, *Real Estate Debt Can Make You Rich*, which is selling so well that McGraw-Hill wants me to write another. I continue to mentor hundreds of people across the country.

> **DEXTIP**
> Build and nurture ongoing relationships with asset managers, bank managers, realtors and lenders to form connections that will make you rich.

By the way, when my book came out, do you think the asset managers at the REO departments at the banks where I bought my houses got a free copy? YOU BET! Even when those asset managers had no property on their REO lists, I kept in touch with them. People who work at the banks are my friends and I talk their language.

The relationships you build in this business are priceless. Building friendships in this part of the market is what it is all about and that is what you must do.

Where Are These Foreclosures Coming From?

When real estate markets are hot, many real estate investors, both new and experienced, buy at retail prices, wait for the house to appreciate then sell. They do it again and again. That process of flipping works well...until it doesn't.

All across the country, investors are now stuck with properties they cannot sell. They will not rent for anywhere close to their payments. Not only are they awash with negative cash flows as sluggish re-sale markets become more common across the country, investors are upside-down in that they owe more than the property is worth.

New investors used to the easy money that the get-rich-quick salesmen promise and landlords new to the multiple property ownership game are not the only ones afflicted by the change in the market. First-time homebuyers, as well as other homeowners, took on too much debt. When real estate values soften in the once white-hot meccas of real estate appreciation, these six most vulnerable segments of the market are most likely to lose their houses:

1. *Poorly qualified first-time homebuyers* who should have remained renters and soon will be again;
2. *Over-encumbered homeowners* using their home equity to maintain a champagne lifestyle;
3. *Under-qualified borrowers put into loans they did not understand, such as* hybrids and option arms. They should have read my book, *Real Estate Debt Can Make You Rich*, and they would have seen the pitfalls of that short-term thinking.
4. *Zealous builders* who cannot sell their new houses even with generous incentives and concessions. Developers are calling auction companies to dispose of unsold inventory and to sell units at their unsuccessful condo conversions. Condo conversions not sold at builders' auctions will go back to the bank (REOs).

Other borrowers who bought earlier in the project start to default as well.

5. *Exotic loan holders* who are part of the $2 trillion in adjustable-rate mortgages that are due to reset (at higher interest rates) in the next eighteen to twenty-four months. What these people are looking at is a 30% to 60% jump in their monthly bill if rates fall; a much bigger payment shock will be in store if they rise.

6. *The Four D's (death, divorce, disease and dis-employment)* happen in good times and bad.

   a. People die and the heirs are distant, broke or estranged. When I see a boarded-up house with weeds growing all around it, many times it is part of an unsettled estate with heirs fighting over money. If there are loan payments due and nobody's got any money to advance to the estate, that property usually becomes a foreclosure.

   b. When there is a divorce, nobody wants to make the payment on a house that is now loaded with much emotional baggage. Acrimonious separations mean house payments don't get made. Most couples rely on both incomes to make the mortgage payments. If one person moves out and leaves the other to make the entire mortgage payment, the property usually ends up in foreclosure. With divorces, everybody loses. Especially the kids.

   c. Unexpected illnesses can produce a big whopper of a medical bill, and are the number one cause of bankruptcies in this country. This is the saddest cause of people losing their houses, particularly when people get older. If they have not planned for higher expenses that old age brings, the house goes back to the bank.

> **DEXTIP**
> Aging Baby Boomers, unprepared for old age, will feed the REO market for years to come.

   d. Recent studies show more Americans feel uncertain about their jobs and are dedicating more and more of their monthly incomes to their house payments. With a declining savings rate in this country, the margin for error becomes slim indeed, especially when unemployment hits.

National Homeownership Rate Is Falling

Loose loan standards have boosted the American homeownership rate to 69.7% in a short time. That is quite an achievement. Despite the REO market being fed for years to come because of easy credit, *four out of five subprime borrowers will keep their houses.*

Even though the newspapers are filled with stories about all the poor homeowners being "preyed upon" by unscrupulous lenders, this U.S. housing boom over the past decade turned about five million renters into homeowners, says William Wheaton, a professor of economics and real estate at the Massachusetts Institute of Technology. But many of the loans that made that possible have proved unsustainable. Dr. Wheaton expects about two-thirds of those people to go back to renting. Eventually, he says, rents will rise, and more people will see owning as a better alternative, helping to revive the housing market, perhaps in 2009 or 2010.

Dr. Wheaton is correct since recent census figures show that the national home ownership rate *declined in Q2 2007 to 68.2% from a peak high of 69.2% in Q2 2004.* Those renters who do not realize the dream of homeownership will help landlords do a ton of business in coming years.

Two Trends Make This Downturn Different

Job losses during recessionary times are the usual reason for real estate downturns. The difference is this cycle is that *it's not the economy that is causing these houses to go upside down. It is more the types of loans:* 100% financing, short-term fixed rate loans and adjustable rate loans (particularly the option ARM adjustable with low start rates). At the end of every cycle, homeowners and speculators turn to these Frankenstein loans, which stretches affordability.

Wall Street investment bankers, mortgage bankers and hedge fund investors have helped create a monster that we have not seen before. The lenders of these non-performing loans don't want them back—providing more opportunity for the astute REO investor.

A second and even more ominous trend is that the American Bankers Association says that these distressed homeowners are, for the first time, *paying their credit cards before their mortgage payments.* During the housing boom, consumers used their home equity to pay daily living expenses. The ABA report says these *consumers are paying the price for reckless attitudes* about debt fostered by years of easy credit, particularly in the mortgage market.

I seem to remember, ten or fifteen years ago, that most people made their house payments, no matter what, so as not to lose their homes. The homes of these new and inexperienced homeowners are going back to the bank, which will stoke this wave of bank foreclosures. No wonder we have a negative savings rate in this country.

Take advantage of these new trends! The focus of this book is to teach you how to ride this train of distress with carloads of REOs that are now arriving into the station. There is nothing better than buying and holding a portfolio of properties bought below market value in times of distress. If you buy a house just a little below market price, your return is magnified because of that intact equity.

Dealing with change makes you stronger and dealing with that change in times of distress makes you wiser. Keeping your financial head while everyone else is losing theirs is what astute real estate investors do.

Why Do Those Borrowers Get Those Frankenstein Loans?

Short-term financing to get the low rates has been raging like a rampant disease. Two groups are stretching to get that house payment as low as possible:

1. Inexperienced investors in search of positive cash flow to buy a house with no money in the deal;
2. New homebuyers with low credit scores, no savings and insufficient income.

They got Frankenstein loans without thinking it through. A house is a long-term asset that usually deserves long-term financing. They thought they could always refinance their way out of trouble, or maybe sell the house if things didn't work out. But, as we all know, trees don't grow to the sky and houses do not go up forever. Those kinds of thinkers are "flashes-in-the-pan" and are not acquainted with how to build long-term wealth.

Frankenstein Loans

These are nothing more than adjustable rate loans (including option ARMs) and short-term fixed-rate hybrid loans (like two-year, five-year and seven-year fixed rate loans). *These loans have been around forever; there is nothing wrong with them, rightly used.* The big problem we have now is these payments are re-adjusting to monster-like proportions. Borrowers don't look at how their payments can double or triple overnight and, what's even worse, the loan industry has failed to educate them. These loans work well for financial sophisticates, not for the woefully ignorant.

Many of these recent arrivals to the housing market have eschewed traditional wisdom, and now they are paying for it. But the fortunate few will suffer through, hang on and eventually get a better loan and keep their houses.

In the story, Frankenstein turned on his creator. We will see how the loan industry has created its own monster.

CHAPTER 3

The Subprime Meltdown Is Bigger Than You Think

How did this come about? I have been following this new phenomenon since it first appeared. As a lender who has been following the money markets for almost two decades, I'll tell you what the hoopla is all about and how all these bad credit loans will affect you.

Subprime loans made to people with low FICO scores (620 or below) have always been around in one form or another. If you had a recent foreclosure or bankruptcy on your credit report, you got a subprime loan. In addition, these loans have all sorts of flexible and unusual guidelines that fit the market place, alternatives to no documentation, appraisal variances and clouds on title, loans made to foreign corporations, third and fourth mortgages and the like.

In short, any borrower who did not conform to the norm could usually find a subprime lender that would fund the loan. But you had to have equity, at least 20%, and the rates were high since subprime loans were known to be risky. And the terms were always short-term and meant to be a band-aid to overcome a temporary problem. There have always been subprime shops, but they historically come and go because of the risky nature of the business.

A new loan came into vogue in the early 2000s. *Alternative A credit loans, or ALT-A loan products*, were born to encompass borrowers with excellent credit who do not quite fit the prime profile. *These loans brought more flexible and unusual guidelines to a new market.* Borrowers may need a higher loan to value (LTV), lack traditional employment (tip earners, seasonal employees, or commissioned workers who lack consistent, verifiable income levels), be individuals with complex financial situations, such as being self-employed, or be borrowers unwilling to provide extensive documentation.

Suddenly, if you wanted to buy investment property with 0% down, you could. If you didn't have a traditional job, low to no documentation was accepted. Not much money in the bank? We can overcome that. Have an unlimited number of investment properties? You can get a loan to buy another one. Want to have unlimited cash out? You can have it. No job? No problem.

Wall Street Money: Leveraging Debt With More Debt

But you had to have good FICO scores, **or at least that was the way it was at first.** Investment bankers on Wall Street packaged all these subprime, ALT-A and prime loans in securitized bundles of debt called collateralized debt obligations (CDOs) or mortgaged backed securities (MBSs). These offered a high yield to fixed income investors (many of whom were from overseas), especially when Wall Street leveraged them with debt. They were leveraging debt with more debt. These MBSs were touted to be safe, almost as safe as the treasury bonds backed by the U.S. government. And these investors even had the added benefit of two well-regarded bond rating agencies (Moody's and Standard and Poor) going through each MBS and rate the debt from the best (AAA) to the junk (BBB-).

But storm clouds gathered on the horizon in late 2006. Some of the low rated junk investors were not receiving their promised stream of income. People started defaulting on their loans These BBB- slices of debt (100% loans, low FICO scores, second and third loans), now called *toxic waste* by some, are of very recent vintage. They stopped performing early on. Per contract, the issuers of these loans had to start buying them back since they were not seasoned and not performing (some of these high-risk borrowers did not make one payment).

> **DEXTIP**
> Distressed REO properties will abound for a long time.

The buy-backs are what have *caused over 220 lenders to go bankrupt or become severely impaired* since late 2006. And now some of the prime and ALT-A lenders are being forced to buy back their debt as well. Some have closed their doors or are wobbly. Investors don't want those bad, non-performing loans or the properties they were lent on.

Lenders went too far out on a limb, lowered FICO score requirements and lent money out on higher and higher LTV loans. Too much faith was placed in the credit scoring model (FICO) that only became popular with lenders in 1997. Never before have we had so many loans written upon the reliability of a credit scoring system that has never gone through a real estate downturn

Because of a national housing market on the skids and interest rates on the rise, the turmoil in the mortgage markets will have profound effects on the economy as a whole.

Subprime Meltdown Spreads: The Far-Reaching Effects of This Sub-Prime Contagion

Sneezing spreads germs. The uninfected party next to you who just got splattered by your sneeze droplets is the recipient of your cold viruses, called *contagions*, as in "contagious."

So it is with this subprime crisis that is now infecting formerly unaffected parts of the economy. Here are thirty-two ways this domino effect impacts all of us:

1. Home prices decline as more people default. It is the first national home price decline since the Great Depression;
2. Most listings in U.S. history;
3. Highest number of empty houses for sale…ever;
4. Neighborhood quality suffers. Boarded-up, foreclosed-on houses can be magnets for crime and be a deterrent for homebuyers and business investors;
5. In neighborhoods with high foreclosures, mosquito infestations have occurred from the backyards' green pools filled with stagnant water;
6. Tax revenues down. Cities will scurry for new sources;
7. Municipal credit ratings suffer;
8. Wall Street brokerages (Bear Sterns, Merrill Lynch) losing much of their value;
9. Lenders tighten, taking liquidity out of the market;
10. Consumer spending down and retail suffers;
11. Less vacation travel as consumers have less money to spend;
12. Higher rates on corporate borrowings;
13. Top ten homebuilder stocks down 35%-50%, reaching 3+ year low;

14. U.S. Securities and Exchange Commission has opened a dozen investigations into high-risk collateralized debt obligations linked to the sinking value of subprime mortgages;
15. Federal and state legislation ban stated on income loans, prepayment penalties and require impound accounts;
16. Credit dries up with increased regulation;
17. Possibly higher interest rates, higher gold prices and a weakening dollar;
18. Global debt meltdown;
19. Global equity markets suffer in all eighteen Western European markets;
20. Record-high vacancy rate for U.S. homes;
21. Remittances down to Mexico and other foreign countries as construction workers get laid off;

Positive Effects:

22. For some, more jobs;
23. A thriving REO market;
24. Banks/asset managers hiring more staff;
25. Banks rehab contractors;
26. Foreclosure tracking services;
27. Foreclosure advisor services for homeowners;
28. Bank real estate brokers get listings;
    You have got to realize there is much more to this recent trend than just buying REO houses. Many are paying the price for those caught unprepared:
29. The next generation of first-time homebuyers;
30. Stated income borrowers with good credit;
31. Landlords benefit because foreclosees will go back to renting houses, thereby increasing rents;
32. Stage is being set for the next up-market.

But the Subprime Meltdown Is Also Smaller Than You Think

Don't go out and slit your wrists because you think I am forecasting economic Armageddon. Let's put things in perspective. Although a large part of the recent buying surge was fueled in part by easy credit, according to the Mortgage Bankers Association, in this ten-trillion-dollar American mortgage market:

1. thirty-five percent of all homeowners own their homes free and clear;
2. fifty percent of all borrowers have long-term fixed rates (five trillion);
3. thirty percent of all the loans out there are prime adjustables (three trillion);
4. thirteen percent are ALT-A (1.3 trillion);
5. seven percent are subprime (700 billion).

The economy will not drop off a cliff, although a little breather is in order. Consumer spending, which has been almost 70% of the economy, will surely diminish. Investment spending by business, buttressed by the global trade, has been soaring

Lenders have eliminated most no-money-down "subprime" loans for people with weak credit records. Stated income loans are also harder to get. That means many people who hoped to buy homes this year will have to wait until they can clean up their credit records and save for a down payment, like in the old days. This will add to future "pent up" demand.

Recent consumer confidence reports are on the upswing. However, at a conference of mortgage lenders, David Lowman, head of the mortgage business at J.P. Morgan Chase & Co., warned: "The largest part of the problem in the subprime space is ahead of us, not behind us." Many borrowers who got loans in the past couple of years are still paying the low initial monthly payments and have yet to face the steeper adjustable rates that kick in after two or three years. Once they do, foreclosures are sure to rise.

Mark Zandt, chief economist of Moody's Economy.com, a research firm in West Chester, PA, *expects lenders to acquire about 900,000 homes this year and roughly the same number next year through foreclosures,* up from an average of about 500,000 a year from 2000 through 2006. That will add to the glut of homes on the market, further depressing prices in some areas.

Homeowners in Trouble Are in Rampant Denial

Many afflicted homeowners stay in complete denial about their situation. Some come to realize that they cannot save their property and do not bother trying. They just abandon the property, bury their heads in the sand and let it go to auction even if they have equity.

Here are the steps they go through trying to save the family castle. They try to:

1. *Come up with the money* to reinstate their loan (reinstating a loan means paying all of the back payments and late fees) and stop the foreclosure.

2. *They try to borrow money from relatives, friends or other sources* but are not able to do so in time. It is amazing how many homeowners think they are going to get a loan from one source or another only to discover too close to the auction date that their sources or credit have dried up.

3. *Refinance the property* only to find out that they do not qualify for a loan because they are in foreclosure. Refinancing means the homeowner applies for a new loan on the house. The new loan would be large enough to pay off the loan that is in foreclosure, plus the reinstatement amount and the foreclosure attorney's fees. ("No way," I have to say to them when they call me for a new loan. They've got to have equity and the interest rates are ugly. Even when they qualify for a new high-interest rate loan, they can't afford those high payments. They soon start sliding down that slippery slope of foreclosure.)

4. *Deed-in-lieu-of-foreclosure.* Hand the property back to the bank and try to work something out to save your credit. Asset managers call this *jingle mail*, when the borrower walks and mails the bank the house keys.

5. *Bankruptcy.* Even with tighter and more restrictive rules and a means test to qualify for bankruptcy, homeowners are still filing for it because it stops the foreclosure, at least for awhile. The bank petitions the bankruptcy court to have the homeowners' property released from bankruptcy protection so they can foreclose. This happens quite often.

6. *Sell and put the property on the market.* Many homeowners try to sell the property before the foreclosure auction, but are unsuccessful because:

    •   They list the property with a Realtor at an unreasonably high price.
    •   They try to sell it themselves (FSBO).
    •   The property is a dog and in poor condition, which makes finding a buyer very difficult.
    •   There is not enough time to sell it before the auction.

- The property has far more debt on it than what it's worth.
- Is not well-located or is far away in the boondocks.
- It has to compete with a lot of other, more desirable properties.
- The property is a condominium that has to compete with a lot of other re-sales in the project.

Short Sales Sometimes Save the Day

If the homeowner sells the property for less than what is owed before it hits the courthouse steps, the lender has agreed to a *short sale*. The home's purchase price is for less than what is owed. At the end of hyper appreciating markets, you see lots of short sales because the banks lent too much money and are now taking it in the shorts.

You would think banks would be eager to get these properties off of their books and at least get some of their money back. *But banks don't think like you and I do.* Their loan servicing may not even be talking to the loss mitigation department (usually the place where short sales are authorized). And the REO departments may not talk with any other department. The bank's organizational structure can be quite dysfunctional. But, as we will see, the bank's inefficiencies can be seeds for opportunities.

A successful short sale usually has a dogged and persistent Realtor's fingerprints all over it. They take a long time, and buyers often walk. Realtors have to hold the transaction together by dealing with unmotivated and busy bank employees, a panicked seller watching his money and credit rating go up in smoke, and an impatient buyer who is seeing better deals all around him.

Credit-wise, a short sale can really mitigate the damage to the seller's credit rating. Once that first bit of paper called a notice of default gets filed, it's over. The credit report's public record section registers a foreclosure. Credit scores plunge, the foreclosure notation stays on the credit report for ten years, and the hapless seller is locked out of the good loans for at least two years.

But with a short sale, the bank has more leeway. Many times a simple entry showing "creditor accepted less than agreed" is all that shows up. Not a great thing to see, but much better than the black mark of a foreclosure. But if nothing can be worked out, the property goes through foreclosure and now the bank gets it

How the Bank Seizes the Collateral

As many of these above property owners cannot make their payments, they will be subject to foreclosure actions by the banks that lent them the money. Every state has a certain foreclosure procedure that is dictated by state statute but basically it works like this: When the homeowner stops making the payment, alarm bells start to go off at the lender's servicing department.

If the due date is missed by thirty days, the homeowner has a thirty-day late mark on their credit report (not good). Banks can start the foreclosure process immediately, but they usually do not (they are waiting longer and longer now). What usually happens is they will start calling and sending all sorts of collection letters. If the homeowner doesn't respond to the increasingly ominous communications and the next house payment is missed, a sixty-day late mark is registered on the credit report (bad).

So after two or more months of no payments, they will file a notice of default, which instigates the foreclosure process. The start of foreclosure proceedings is a matter of public record, which shows up on the borrower's credit report for ten years (terrible). This NOD is sent to the defaulting homeowner.

After a time, if nothing is done, the lender will send a public notice of sale (NOS) letting the hapless property owner and now the whole world know that the property will be auctioned off at the courthouse steps. At the auction, the property can be bought by the highest bidder. If no bids are attracted to the property, the lender takes possession of the collateral and becomes the new owner.

Sometimes the Loan Is Guaranteed by Another Entity

Many loans are insured against loss by the Veterans Administration (VA), the Federal Home Loan Administration (FHA) or a private mortgage insurance company (MI). Many other governmental agencies, like the Small Business Administration (SBA), the United States Department of Agriculture (USDA) and others, have loan guarantee programs to promote homeownership. But the VA and the FHA are the most common.

The banks still fund the loan but they will not lose more than 80% of the money they lent. In this case, that entity gets first dibs on the property and they may take it back so they can recoup their investment. If they do exercise this option, then you have to deal with them. I have had very good luck buying from the VA.

After the Foreclosure Auction: Vandals and Squatters

Sometimes the owner wants to ride it to the very end and still reside in the property. The former owner now becomes a tenant and the bank is the owner/landlord. By now the bank will probably have retained a real estate agent who is now the manager of the bank's asset. Offering cash for the keys to the house is usually the first move. If they cannot buy the foreclosee out, the eviction process starts.

I have seen some very ugly bank evictions when the former homeowner trashes the place: holes in the wall, lawn's dead, lighting fixtures gone and animal feces all over. Countertops can get stripped, faucets and showerheads disappear and even the copper wiring/plumbing gets stolen. And the neighbors sometimes join in. It is not unusual to see air conditioning compressors and landscaping items end up in the neighbors' backyards. I have looked over the fences at some of the repossessed property and seen these items magically appear.

Some evictees will prolong their inevitable exit even longer by filing what is called a *bare-bones bankruptcy*. The bankruptcy will never be completed; it is only meant to delay the process for a little bit longer. It is an effective stall tactic.

Needles and Liquor Bottles
Empty, bank foreclosed houses are a blight for the neighborhood. Dead, yellowed lawns and ratty-looking houses pull a neighborhood down. I have seen homeless vagrants trash a house, leaving used hypodermic needles and liquor bottles in their wake.

Too many vacant houses in the neighborhood are dangerous for everybody, including the bank (which is a great negotiating tool for you to tell the banks when you want to buy the house).

Boarded Up Houses Are Bad for Everybody
If experiences from the housing dip of the '90s and recent studies are any barometer, even homeowners sitting pretty with their own mortgages should be concerned about vacant houses. Houses get boarded up because windows get broken into by tramps. There's nothing like a few of these to scare off buyers when the neighbors are trying to sell their residences.

Crimes Jump 6.7%
Every time a neighborhood experiences 2.8 foreclosures out of 100 owner-occupied properties in a single year, crime there and in the surrounding blocks jumps 6.7%, according to a 2006 census tract study by the Georgia Institute of Technology and the Chicago-based Woodstock Institute.

One REO Slices 1% off the Value of Every House in the Neighborhood

A related study by the same researchers concluded that homeowners lose 0.9% of their property value if they are within one-eighth of a mile from a conventionally foreclosed-on, single-family residence. A $500,000 home, for example, would drop by $4,500.

The value of your property is tied to the ability to sell it, and if somebody comes to your block and sees a battered-looking property across the street with boarded-up windows, that has an exponential impact. In densely packed communities, a concentration of foreclosures makes it even harder for other homes to sell.

Since I am in the lending business, I speak the bank's language. They want to know the condition of the property and the looks of the neighborhood so I have had the fortune of them letting me go out and report back about the damage. REOs happen every time in boom markets where investors think trees will grow to the sky. There is an old saying that pigs get rich while hogs get slaughtered. Pigs feast in times of market distress by BUYING LOW and HOLDING HIGH.

Loan Modifications Add to More Slow-Motion Foreclosures

The banks these days are a lot more amenable if they are contacted and something is worked out. They have entire staffs in their loss mitigation departments specifically trained to help defaulting borrowers become current. Lenders are loathe to have their balance sheets filled with non-performing assets (REOs), so they start *doing loan modifications* or what I call *slow-motion foreclosures*.

Since the lenders are destined to be running bloated REO departments these days, they are trying to modify the loans to keep the homeowners in the houses. Lenders are increasingly:

1. *Changing at least one term of the mortgage.* It is used to bring the loan current by capitalizing on the delinquent interest, extending the fixed period on an ARM loan or lowering the interest.
2. *Offering repayment plans.* A formal, written agreement in which delinquent borrowers pledge to bring their loan up to date within a limited amount of time, usually less than eighteen months. This is often used by borrowers who have had serious setbacks, such as illnesses, injuries or temporary layoffs, that will most likely not be repeated.

3. *Entering into forbearance agreements.* This is when the lender reduces or suspends payments for a specific period of time, usually no more than three months. It's a useful strategy for people who have experienced a catastrophe such as a natural disaster, short-term illness, or short-term unemployment, or if there is a pending sale of the property. The suspended payments are added on to the loan.

4. *Agreeing to take the property back via a deed-in-lieu-of-foreclosure.* If there's not enough home equity to yield a profit, lenders may accept this option, which results in no exchange of cash. The homeowner simply turns over ownership to the lender and walks away. The borrower preserves more creditworthiness than if the home is foreclosed on.

The reason I call these agreements slow-motion foreclosures is because most people don't catch up once they are behind the eight ball. *Lenders agree with me that once a person comes out of this loss mitigation process, they usually go back in.*

At a bank REO conference, one loss mitigator said that her company was experiencing a 200% increase in foreclosures and 32% of those were in loss mitigation at some point.

CHAPTER 4

Are You in Foreclosure or Facing It? Is This You?

If you are on the wrong end of this foreclosure process, I have some advice for you. If you overpaid for a property and are now upside down, if you were trying to flip an investment property and got caught by plunging prices, or if you got smooth-talked by an unethical mortgage broker into a bad loan that is going to blow up on you, then you need to hear this.

Perhaps you have refinanced your credit card debt while re-doing your home loan and you are still barely making it. Maybe you are a newbie and it is tough finding out you are not a great landlord, your tenants are running you ragged and you are not cut out for the buy-and-hold property game.

In any case, it's time to face facts. You screwed up, and you are going to lose your property—and your money. *If this is you, don't worry. It happened to me.* First we are going to talk about you, and then we are going to talk about the banks.

Be honest:

1. **Can you truly afford to live where you live?** Many people I mentor cannot keep up with their cost of living and they're not making the income to support themselves. Californians in particular have trouble keeping up with a higher cost of living, and it is getting higher all the time. Did you know that the inflation rate

in California is usually one percentage point higher than that of the rest of the country? California has always been a high cost state, and the price of paradise rises faster than those in other parts of the country. Maybe you need to move out of the state to more affordable areas, as many are doing right now. Maybe you need to rent for awhile until you get on your financial feet.

2. **Did you buy in an area you are not familiar with?** Many investors, attracted to cheaper houses outside their area, are finding *that out-of-state, low-priced glitter is not gold.* They are running into declining markets, properties that are staying vacant longer and low rents. Did you get a bad loan? How long can you hold on to those negative cash flow alligators?

> **DEXTIP**
> Next time, buy property locally; there are diamonds in your backyard.

3. **Were you going for the quick kill?** There is nothing like holding houses you can't sell or rent. You've got to be really good to buy and quickly re-sell property for profit. In appreciating markets, it is easy to make money. But when the tide goes out and properties are not going up anymore, then you get to see, as Warren Buffet says, who has been swimming naked.

I know some of the best buy/sell guys in the business, and you've got to buy really low or the carrying costs will eat you up. If you want to flip REOs for profit, I have a chapter just for you later in this book.

People Facing Foreclosure Are Not in Their Right Minds

Siege mentalities develop when you lose your house. Every day you wake up in your home bunker waiting to bailed out, hoping the next loan will come through, the market will change, the property will sell or the market will improve. It doesn't help that you might have an amateur vulture, like I was, darkening your front door or sending you a bunch of postcards.

Are you an ostrich or an owl? Denial sets in when you get that far behind in your payments. Don't be an ostrich and bury your head in the sand; be a wise owl and look around for solutions. Most importantly, contact your lender and see if those five solutions above work for you. You just may save your house, or at least lessen the damage to your credit.

I was responsible for my foreclosure, and so are you. Do not fall into bad financial habits. Be an astute real estate investor. Astute investors:

1. take advantage of buying opportunities when the market changes;
2. never lose sight of their long-range goals;
3. use debt wisely.

A California Story of Excess From Dr. Housing Bubble (www.drhousingbubble.com)

We all know that foreclosures are on the rise throughout the nation. Most people realize that a foreclosure means that you will lose your home. But how does this process look?

In reality, the foreclosure process is a drawn out and lengthy ordeal. It is a gut-wrenching and personal nightmare for most folks. So this is a story about a couple that is the poster representation of the housing boom and bust. In this article, we will examine their professions, incomes and monthly budget. Amazingly, folks are very upfront when they are making lots of money but go into clandestine mode when they are having financial difficulties. Below is the couple's profile:

Joe and Mary

- Ages: 29 and 28
- Professions: Joe—senior account executive (lender); Mary—real estate agent
- Home purchase: Costa Mesa 4/2 home, bought in late 2004 for $675,000
- Location: Orange County
- Yearly income combined: $130,000 gross
- Net monthly income (after taxes): $8,200
- Automobiles: Mercedes E350 Sedan ($599/33-month lease), GL 450 SUV (purchase $56,000)
- Monthly auto fuel cost (filling up once per week): $350
- Credit card Ddbt: $25,000
- Monthly food budget (including dining out): $700

This should give you a nice snapshot of the couple. Since they were sophisticated investors in the know, they decided to jump into the home with a 2/28 loan, interest only with no money down. After all, two people making $130,000 a year can clearly sustain pretty much anything, right? And, as we all know, "no money down" was no longer simply a thing of late-night infomercials but a mainstream way of buying a home. Here is the monthly budget with the teaser rate loan (they had it for 2.75%):

2004 Budget

- House payment (PITI at 2.75% interest only/2 years): $2,249
- Auto cost (monthly payment/lease/loan/fuel): $1,749
- Dining: $700
- Credit card payment: $500

Total:	**$5,198**
Monthly net:	**$8,200**
Disposable income:	*$3,002*

Keep in mind we are not factoring in medical insurance, cell phone costs, utility bills, retirement accounts, and many other items. These are things that I am aware of regarding their budget, since I was privy to the information. Well, it was more like they were showing off to me, but I made mental notes on these items as I would with past clients showing me their monthly budgets.

So, even with that said, $3,002 a month in disposable income is a pretty nice chunk of change to pay for the remaining monthly items. But, again, this was a teaser 2/28 loan. Unfortunately, they didn't factor in one of them losing his job, a rate reset, and a slumping housing market. Let us take a look at the late 2006 monthly budget:

2006 Budget

- House payment (PITI amortized fully over 28 years/full rate of 6.25%): $4,962
- Auto cost (monthly payment/lease/loan/fuel): $1,749
- Dining: $700
- Credit card payment: $500

Total:	**$7,911**
Monthly net:	**$8,200**
Disposable income:	*$289*

Suddenly, the jump in the rate creates a crunch on the household income. Keep in mind that the above still doesn't factor in other monthly costs. In addition, this was in late 2006, before Joe lost his senior accounting job because the company went under. They were already feeling the pinch since the housing industry was showing signs of weakness and their incomes, being variable with commissions, were also taking a hit. Joe jumped to another mortgage outfit but they were only able to give him $30,000 a year base plus any commissions.

Of course, with the tightening of the housing market, business was not going so well since both of their careers were tied directly to the housing industry. Their combined incomes are no longer $130,000 a year but approximately $80,000 a year. So let us run the numbers again with the new household income:

2007 Budget

- House payment (PITI amortized fully over 28 years/full rate of 6.25%): $4,962
- Auto cost (monthly payment/lease/loan/fuel): $1,749
- Dining: $700
- Credit card payment: $500

Total:	**$7,911**
Monthly net:	**$5,804**
Disposable income:	*-$2,107*

Now, they are running massive monthly budget deficits. It may come to a shock to many people that a household formerly earning $130,000 a year may actually have financial difficulties. But you can see how easily and quickly someone can go into financial ruin.

Statistically, this couple was in the *top ten percent of household incomes in the country*. Yet they spent way beyond their means. California living is very expensive. You'll also notice that by being in the industry they are in, they felt that they needed symbols of affluence to keep up with the Joneses. So now you can see that it was not only folks who made $14,000 a year purchasing $720,000 that got into mortgage trouble; even those considered the most affluent also have financial problems. The next phase of this case study is the foreclosure process.

Foreclosure had been a somewhat novel, unheard of thing in California for the past decade. Any homeowners in trouble were able to put their homes up for sale and they would sell quickly before the entire process ran its course. The market was so hot that it covered financial irresponsibility by letting folks off the hook. This all ended last year.

Nightmare Scenario

- House payments going up and up;
- Property worth less;
- No equity;
- Gotta sell.

Suddenly, the market is declining, yet rates are still resetting. People are realizing that they are unable to make the payments or sell for their asking price, and are losing their homes. So how did Joe and Mary lose their home? This is the next stage of the foreclosure story, and it is a sad one.

The psychology of running massive monthly deficits is a hard one, especially for outsiders. For one, many readers are probably wondering about the incredibly high car cost. This is Southern California and having a new model is somewhat common practice. However, *the worst depreciating item you can own is a vehicle.* Regardless, Mary and Joe purchased one of their two Mercedes and, after a year or so, if they decided to sell, they would be selling at a loss. So after Joe lost his job, they decided to put their home up for sale, knowing they would be unable to make the payments. At first, they thought that they would be able to make a nice profit on the home. This was not the case. This is how the following months looked:

Months 1-3 (Pre-foreclosure)

Joe and Mary miss one payment. They have their home listed at $790,000 on the MLS. No bites. The bank sends a late notice. Since they've been in the industry, they have seen homes sell even before landing on the MLS. They are certain that they will sell their home.

Total monthly payment behind:	$4,962
Late payment:	$40
Total to cure account:	**$5,002**

Another month goes by and no offers. They lower the price to $775,000 to generate some interest. Nothing. They start getting a bit anxious. They get another notice from the bank but, this time, they will need to make two payments. At this point, they make a conscious decision not to pay the mortgage and put in a clause for a future buyer to cure the account when they buy.

Total monthly payment behind: $9,924
Late payment: $40 x 2
Total to cure account: **$10,004**

At this point the bank tries to make contact with Joe and Mary. If they couldn't pay $5,002, how were they going to pay double that? A third month comes along and they lower the home price to $750,000. Still, the market is dry and silent. At this point the couple receives formal letters from the bank and its attorney.

Total monthly payment behind: $14,886
Late payment: $40 x 3
Legal fees: $75
Total to cure account: **$15,081**

Month 4:

Total monthly payment behind: $19,848
Late payment: $40 x 4
Legal fees: $75 x 2
Total to cure account: **$20,158**

Month 5:

Total monthly payment behind: $24,810
Late payment: $40 x 5
Legal fees: $75 x 3
Total to cure account: **$25,160**

The bank issues a demand for full payment, including full balance, back interest, late charges and legal fees, all at once. The legal notices come. Joe and Mary now have their home listed at $715,000. Still no bites. They did have some people come by but the deals didn't materialize. Now they need $25,160 to cure the account but the bank has legally informed them that they will accept no payments except a full balance payment on their original $675,000 note. Keep in mind that the bank is no place for negotiations. Can you imagine calling up your local Mercedes dealer and saying, "Hello, Mercedes? Yeah, I'm not going to be able to afford the $600 this month but would you be willing to take $300 plus a free Dodgers ticket?"

The bank now sends a certified letter of notice of intent to foreclose. Joe and Mary realize they will not sell their home. The notice and waiting period begins. They stay in the place two more months. Now it will cost $35,000+ to bring the account current, plus a full payment on the balance. Of course this will never happen given the circumstances of their finances. No payments are arranged and the house is sold at auction and, of course, the bank reclaims the home as REO since the Joe and Mary are on the sheets for $675,000.

The home is now officially REO and—get this—they have it listed for $750,000! The bank is delusional. Joe and Mary now have a foreclosure on their credit record and rent a much smaller home. They managed to break the lease on the Mercedes but are on the hook for the purchased SUV.

You'll notice how things spiral out of control when you spend more than you earn. I can only imagine households with $60,000 getting into this mess. If anything, it will accelerate ten times faster. Joe and Mary are considering bankruptcy but the new laws are now more stringent in terms of letting people completely off the hook, especially a couple that makes nearly twice the median U.S. income.

Hopefully this scenario gives you an inside look at the story of foreclosure and how it can happen to anyone. I've seen many blogs address foreclosures and the numbers, but haven't seen a post detailing the entire process and how it impacts a homeowner's bottom line.

It is essential for you to understand that we are in a bubble so large that missing one payment puts you in arrears for $10,000, or the down payment of a modest home in many states. If this is what's already happening in stage one of the bubble, what do you see happening in the later stages?

CHAPTER 5

How Far Down Will Prices Go?

The process I am about to describe may seem extreme to you in the dramatic way I write about it. Just know the more volatile your local real estate market is, the truer this description is.

Just like any business, real estate goes through predictable market cycles. Bank foreclosures appear after a period of *speculative euphoria*. When properties are hyper-appreciating, loans are easy to get and everyone is **thrilled to buy**. Bragging about how much money you made and how much phantom equity you have accrued becomes the subject of many conversations around the water cooler or at cocktail parties. Just buy a house and wait for it to go up: It doesn't require much skill. Anybody can do it.

In hot markets, banks are passing around money like candy and come up with ever more aggressive loan programs to feed the demand and keep the property payments affordable. Hybrid loans with low start rates, adjustable rates and option ARMs that banks are promoting offer liquidity to the market and keep payments low. Lenders will lower guidelines to make loans easier to get, which further increases buyer demand. **Easy money stokes *the buying frenzy*.**

But as properties are priced higher, they become less affordable. Ever more expensive properties are now out-of-sync with local demand. Prices top out and then stagnate for a time before they start their downward slide. *In-denial* real estate salespeople, local economic pundits, homeowners and banks all proclaim that the market will come back shortly—just keep buying.

But the market doesn't come back. Listing times expand, properties stay on the market longer and builders start offering generous incentives and concessions to move into their newly built homes. Sellers find it harder to sell their houses because now they have to compete with new houses that have all the latest amenities.

Most buyers will not buy if they think their high-priced house will be worth less next year. You need more than just a healthy buy and demand component to make for a balanced real estate market. You also need the psychology of positive buyer confidence. All three ingredients have to go into this pot of price appreciation stew.

Bank foreclosures begin to flood the market as ***panicked and desperate*** buyers start missing their payments. All the foreclosed properties that don't get bid on at the courthouse steps because they are upside down (the loan is more than the worth of the property) go back to the banks, so their REO inventory balloons. Banks, whose balance sheets become encumbered with all these non-performing assets, start pulling back and loans become harder to get. Sales slow, everybody stays put and renters keep renting.

Landlords celebrate as families of foreclosed houses need places to rent and flippers sweat it out because first-time homebuyers can't get financing. Rents keep rising as buy/sell guys find another line of work.

 Newspaper headlines trumpet the blood on the streets. Financially strapped sellers feel the heat and ***start capitulating***: they dump their property at any price before they lose everything. Foreclosed houses and bank REO inventories lead the price spiral down, forcing private sellers to chop their prices just to compete.

It's hard to buy property when everybody's down on it. Here are the top ten reasons your friends and family will tell you not to pull the trigger:

1. Real estate will never come back.
2. You are going to lose money.
3. Interest rates are too high.
4. Prices are too high and are going down further.
5. It is hard to get a loan.
6. You can't afford those payments.
7. Too much negative cash flow.
8. That property is too beat up.
9. You will never be able to rent it out.
10. You should have bought ten years ago.

You will never really know the exact market bottom until you have passed it. But the trends you will see are declining foreclosures and sales activity picking up. As these trends start to take hold, funny things start to happen. The long-forgotten first-time homebuyer emerges. The starter couple will form a new household because their rent has been increasing this whole time while wages have been inflating.

Properties are suddenly perceived to be more affordable and that house payment is not so much more than area rents. *Hopeful first-timers and bottom-fishing investors* start buying at a slow pace that starts to become a trend. People become **optimistic** about real estate again: sales increase, inventory constricts, foreclosures decline and properties sell quicker.

Thus starts the next upsurge in price appreciation. Real estate regains its investment luster, new gurus come to town with their can't-lose real estate projects and first-timers enter the market and get their pass at the real estate golden ring

Does This Cycle Happen Everywhere?

Yes, but the boom/bust cycle is less intense in areas of low job growth and moderate population inflow. The less economic vibrancy in an area, the less the local real estate cycle is prone to violent swings. Price appreciation is likely to be light because of low demand for housing in the Midwest and parts of the South.

The following chart shows what National City/Global Insight estimates to be the most undervalued metropolitan areas of the United States. These areas are now attracting domestic in-migration from homeowners and investors seeking affordable housing. Despite this recent interest, foreclosure statistics still show very high default rates, probably because there is a lot of land to build on and there are lower median income levels.

MOST UNDERVALUED METRO AREAS
Where to find the best bargains

CITY	STATE	MEDIAN HOME PRICE	PERCENT UNDERVALUED
Dallas	TX	$133,800	24.9%
Houston	TX	$117,600	22.1%
College Station	TX	$103,300	22.1%
Ft. Worth	TX	$110,400	21.2%
Rochester	NY	$113,600	19.5%
Indianapolis	IN	$134,400	16.6%
Kileen	TX	$104,600	16.4%
Witchita	KS	$99,100	16.3%
Lafayette	IN	$113,400	16.2%
Tulsa	OK	$102,200	15.9%
Lubbock	TX	$83,700	14.8%

Source: National City Corp/Global Insight

Another reason that there is likely to be a continued surge in REOs in these areas is the huge amounts of subprime loans as well as more exotic option ARM loans that were sold there in the years 2005-2006.

These markets are said to be *linear markets*, in which appreciation has been slow to non-existent in the past. There will probably be a slower bounce back in prices (if they go down at all), if history proves correct.

Contrast that chart with this next one. Most of these areas have seen such a run-up in price that Global Insight says these are the most overvalued cities in the

Global Insight says these areas are most prone for a price hit. Most are cities in coastal states where there has been high job growth and rampant investor speculation. Supply constraints also drive price appreciation in many of these areas.

I call these *cyclical* markets.

MOST OVERVALUED METRO AREAS
Where housing prices are most out of line

CITY	STATE	MEDIAN HOME PRICE	PERCENT OVERVALUED
Bend	OR	$324,400	78.7%
Prescott	OR	$246,600	64.6%
Naples	FL	$383,300	63.4%
Merced	CA	$280,900	63.2%
Madera	CA	$314,100	62.9%
Miami	FL	$309,200	59.2%
Atlantic City	NJ	$272,100	57.8%
San Bernardino	CA	$346,400	56.7%
Salinas	CA	$596,900	56.3%
Flagstaff	AZ	$274,900	55.6%

Source:National City Corp/Global Insight

country. The thinking goes that since they had such a big run-up, these metro areas are heading for a big fall.

Magnificent opportunities to buy bank foreclosures are to be had since most of these cities have the highest subprime loan concentration in the country, as well as rampant investor speculation, and are overbuilt.

House prices are clearly unaffordable given the income that the locals are making. But there are a lot of jobs in most of these areas, and income growth is also there. Even though most of these cities are crowded and congested, and there is a stable demand for houses, buyers are scared and many are leaving these areas.

Since these escapees sought more affordable house payments by getting option ARM loans, bank foreclosures surged as these borrowers took on too

---

DEXTIP
Buying bank foreclosures *before* people move back to an area is a stupendous wealth-building strategy for the astute real estate investor.

much debt and could not withstand their payments adjusting up 200% to 300%; with no appreciation, there is not enough equity to refinance. They are losing their houses simply because they chose the wrong kind of loan.

If history proves correct and surrounding states get to be more expensive, people move back because of jobs and lifestyle benefits. Better housing affordability brings people back. They start feeling hopeful and optimistic that the housing boom will restart.

CHAPTER 6

Why This Boom in Bank REOs Will Last Longer Than Most People Think

It's a new era in loan modifications. As defaults on home loans mount, mortgage companies are scrambling to work out deals to help as many borrowers as possible stay in their houses. The loan modifications in lenders' loss mitigation departments become big business.

Loan Modifications Mean More Lenders Will Lose Money More Slowly

On the surface, it seems an obvious tactic. Lenders usually end up losing money on foreclosed homes because of legal and other costs, in addition to the need to sell those properties quickly, often at a knockdown price. Also, politicians are pressing mortgage companies to minimize the damages foreclosures cause to families and neighborhoods. For the last several years, Wall Street investment bankers have sold off mortgage-backed securities (MBSs). These MBSs have funded the highest percentage of home loans in American history.

The $6 trillion market has been shaken recently by losses on some of the riskier types of mortgage bonds—the subprime and Alt-A loans. Because of the way these securities are sold, these efforts can pit groups of holders against each other.

When borrowers can't keep up, lenders typically consider whether it makes sense to offer a *loan modification*. Such workout deals, known as "mods," often involve lowering the interest rate or stretching out the term. Lenders have used mods for years, and the practice is expected to proliferate as defaults rise.

Loan Modifications Are Exploding

Investors holding mortgage-backed bonds are watching nervously because mods may not always be in their best interest. Some investors fear that loan servicers—the firms, often owned by lenders that collect payments and deal with defaults—will make too many mods. Generally, investors favor mods that ease a normally reliable borrower through a rough patch, but not those that merely buy time for deadbeats. Some of these investors doubt that the homeowners even merit a rescue plan. They fear that by making these people current, they are pushing losses to another year or so.

Credit Suisse analysts recently examined loans that had been modified over the past few years by one nationwide lender and found that borrowers missed at least one monthly payment after a mod in *nearly 40% of the cases.* Loss mitigation managers report that at least half of the borrowers fail in their re-payment plan. If the borrower is unlikely to keep up with payments even after a mod, many investors would prefer that servicers pursue a foreclosure quickly, especially in regions where house prices are falling, reducing the value of the collateral.

Servicers are required by their contracts to act in the interests of the investors and modify loans only when that tactic can be expected to reduce losses. That puts servicers in the tricky position of trying to figure out which borrowers are basically sound and when it makes more sense to foreclose quickly.

This Ain't Your Parents' Mortgage Market: Wall Street Rules the Day...And It Is in Trouble

We went over the subprime meltdown thoroughly in previous chapters. Now, let's talk about how this mortgage market in turmoil will benefit savvy REO buyers. Just follow me on this.

When loans go bad, one complication is that different classes of investors have different interests, reflecting the complex mechanics of mortgage securities. These investors *own the loan* so only they can make the call to modify the loan, authorize the short sale or negotiate price to liquidate their collateral if it goes REO. Issues of mortgage-backed securities are divided into slices called *tranches,* with various ratings, depending on the level of risk.

Holders of the highest-rated slices (those with the lowest risk) are first in line to collect payments of interest and principal flowing from the loans. Many such bond issues are structured so that there is initially more than enough cash flow available to cover obligations to all of the investors, leaving a cushion to cover potential losses from loan defaults. If, after three years or so, the loans have performed well enough to meet certain performance measures, the cushion may be reduced.

In that case, some of the excess cash available goes to holders of lower-rated securities and "residuals," the highest-risk parts of the securities that are last in line for payments. If loan mods delay the onset of foreclosures, holders of the lower-rated securities and residuals are more likely to get those payments. But holders of AAA and other high-rated securities may argue that the loan mods have artificially boosted the performance of the loans and that the holders of lower-rated securities and residuals are getting payments that should be preserved to protect owners of higher-rated paper against the risk of a resurgence of defaults later.

Even when there are no clashes among investors, servicers face restrictions on how they modify loans. Many investors are losing money big-time, and are now suing the issuers of these securities. Firms like Morgan Stanley and Merrill Lynch are being sued by these investors, many of whom are from overseas, because these securities were supposed to be safer.

Moody's Investors Service, a ratings provider, recently reviewed roughly 400 subprime mortgage-security transactions issued last year: 5% of those deals prohibit any kind of loan mod; among those that allow mods, about a third stipulate that no more than 5% of the loans backing the securities can be modified.

Either way, a bad loan is likely to take longer to hit the bank's REO department. It may even be hard to determine exactly who owns the loan. Houses can be hot potatoes, passed back and forth from lender to investor to asset manager.

Loan Servicers' Hands Are Tied
As They Become More Inefficient

Lots of restrictions prevent servicers from doing the things they need to do. Since even they do not know if they can make loan modifications or make a deal for a short sale, I think we will see many more slow-motion foreclosures. Despite the effort of loan servicers to work with defaulting borrowers, their hands will become increasingly tied. And in the cases where they can modify the terms on a bad loan, almost one half of those borrowers will end up losing their houses.

The bottom line is that slow-motion foreclosures will probably feed the REO market for a long time. Empty houses slowly disintegrate, which is an added benefit for the astute real estate investor since these inefficiencies are likely to benefit REO investors for years to come as more properties fall through the cracks.

One benefit to the persistent real estate investor is being able to follow properties that fall through the cracks. We will explore some novel ways to follow a property from NOD to REO in later chapters. I predict a vibrant shadow market where properties will suddenly appear in a bank's bloated inventory and will need to be dumped fast. *Astute real estate investors will have the chance to find properties when nobody else is looking.*

Inefficiencies at the Bank to Be Exploited

1. Who owns the note?
2. Files get lost;
3. Compliance issues cause litigation;
4. Chaos at the store;
5. Unsuccessful loss mitigators;
6. Properties are not marketable;
7. Condo glut;
8. Hanging wires and ripped up drywall.

Who Owns the Note?

Judges in at least five states have stopped foreclosure proceedings because the banks that pool mortgages into securities and the companies that collect monthly payments haven't been able to prove they own the mortgages.

Those loans may be sold several times before they land in a security. Mortgage servicers, who collect monthly payments and distribute them to securities investors, can buy and sell the home loans many times. Each time the mortgages change hands, the sellers are required to sign over the mortgage notes to the buyers.

In the rush to originate more loans during the U.S. mortgage boom from 2003 to 2006, that assignment of ownership wasn't always properly completed because the loans were mass produced and shortcuts were taken.

Then the servicing company has to file a "lost note affidavit" to try to prove it to the judge. The home-loan industry has had a central electronic database since 1997 to track mortgages as they are bought and sold. It's run by Mortgage Electronic Registration System, or MERS, a subsidiary of MERSCORP Inc., based in Vienna, VA, and owned by mortgage companies.

No Tracking Mechanism

According to R.K. Arnold, MERS' CEO, the company has 3,246 member companies and about half of outstanding mortgages are registered with them, including loans purchased by government-sponsored entities Fannie Mae, Freddie Mac and Ginnie Mae.

For about half of U.S. mortgages, there is no tracking mechanism.

MERS' rules don't allow members to submit lost-note affidavits in place of mortgage notes. A lot of companies say the note is lost, even when it's highly unlikely.

Nation Doomed to Two Million Foreclosures

One independent researcher, HomePredictor.com, says we are just starting the foreclosure surge:

1. More than **two million homeowners will face foreclosure** in the next two and a half years, due largely to loans that shouldn't have been written.
2. Seventy-six percent of recent foreclosures resulted from high-interest rate subprime loans that were made to borrowers who could not otherwise qualify for a loan.
3. Another fifteen percent of the failed loans were made with conventional mortgages, but many contained risky low- or no-down payment terms.
4. The remaining nine percent of foreclosed loans studied included no- and low-documentation loans that get approved with little if any verification of income.
5. More than fifty percent of all home mortgages made in 2006 were written with five percent or less down.

What Areas Got Them and Who's Got the Most?

You will notice that out of the top ten states, five of them (Colorado, Michigan, Indiana, Ohio and Illinois) had high foreclosure rates in 2006 because of:

1. Weak job growth
2. Low population inflow/people leaving the state
3. Very high concentration of subprime loans.

The other five states (Georgia, Nevada, Texas, Florida and Utah) have high foreclosure rates for other reasons. Buyers have flooded these areas because of job growth and affordable housing. Foreclosures are exploding in these areas because of:

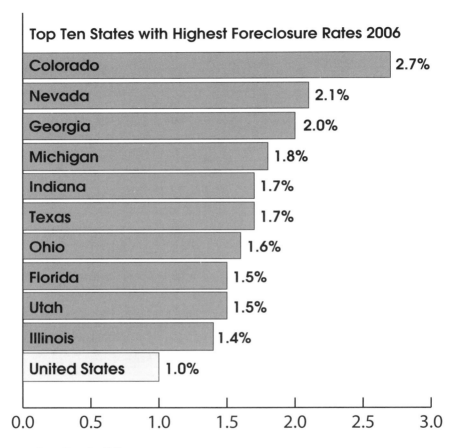

Top Ten States with Highest Foreclosure Rates 2006

State	Rate
Colorado	2.7%
Nevada	2.1%
Georgia	2.0%
Michigan	1.8%
Indiana	1.7%
Texas	1.7%
Ohio	1.6%
Florida	1.5%
Utah	1.5%
Illinois	1.4%
United States	1.0%

1. Overbuilding
2. Lots of vacant land
3. Investor speculation
4. California out-migrants looking for more affordable house payments
5. One hundred percent financing loans
6. Frankenstein loans
7. Very high concentration of subprime loans

California Will Have More REOs Than Any Other State

California now leads the country. Lower interest rates coupled with lenders lowering their underwriting guidelines have made it very easy for marginal buyers to purchase their first homes. Homeowners with bad credit have also used these loans to refinance their equity up to 100% LTV in many cases. At least one out of five of these loans made in 2005-2006 will end in foreclosure.

In some of California's newer housing additions in Sacramento, Bakersfield and Modesto, for example, subprime concentration has been as high as 80%.

Builders that were attracting first-timers and speculators are now experiencing housing additions filled with "for sale" signs and vacant houses. *Lenders are now finding their California REO lists filled with real estate in the Upper Central Valley, Sacramento, San Diego and the Inland Empire.*

Other subprime loan-saturated areas of coastal and central Florida, the Dallas- Fort Worth corridor, coastal Texas and the upper Great Lakes will be prime hunting grounds for bank foreclosures.

The increase in bad loans that are going to foreclosure in California is staggering. When you look at the following chart, keep in mind that about nine in ten houses auctioned at the courthouse steps revert back to the banks. Last year it was maybe one in ten!

NODS County/Region	2006Q4	2007Q4	%Chg	NOS County/Region	2006Q4	2007Q4	%Chg
Los Angeles	4,586	10,393	126.6%	Los Angeles	287	2,581	799.3%
Orange	1,255	2,984	137.8%	Orange	110	821	646.4%
San Diego	1,778	4,383	146.5%	San Diego	292	1,714	487.0%
Riverside	2,287	6,648	190.7%	Riverside	281	2,509	792.9%
San Bernardino	1,839	5,141	179.6%	San Bernardino	137	1,489	986.9%
Ventura	452	1,059	134.3%	Ventura	37	316	754.1%
SoCal*	12,271	30,828	151.2%	SoCal Total*	1,152	9,504	725.0%
San Francisco	127	257	102.4%	San Francisco	9	49	444.4%
Alameda	649	1,612	148.4%	Alameda	69	480	595.7%
Contra Costa	725	2,316	219.4%	Contra Costa	62	778	1154.8%
Santa Clara	530	1,275	140.6%	Santa Clara	38	256	573.7%
San Mateo	222	463	108.6%	San Mateo	17	97	470.6%
Marin	58	118	103.4%	Marin	6	25	316.7%
Solano	350	1,065	204.3%	Solano	36	324	800.0%
Sonoma	202	462	128.7%	Sonoma	18	163	805.6%
Napa	47	128	172.3%	Napa	3	34	1033.3%
Bay Area	2,910	7,696	164.5%	Bay Area Total	258	2,206	755.0%
Santa Cruz	73	155	112.3%	Santa Cruz	13	46	253.8%
Santa Barbara	147	434	195.2%	Santa Barbara	16	137	756.3%
San Luis Obispo	79	208	163.3%	San Luis Obispo	4	52	1200.0%

NODS County/Region	2006Q4	2007Q4	%Chg	NOSCounty/Region	2006Q4	2007Q4	%Chg
Monterey	128	483	277.3%	Monterey	8	154	1825.0%
Coast	427	1,280	199.8%	Coast Total	41	389	848.8%
Sacramento	1,352	3,840	184.0%	Sacramento	175	1,662	849.7%
San Joaquin	604	1,983	228.3%	San Joaquin	64	785	1126.6%
Placer	276	627	127.2%	Placer	29	220	658.6%
Kern	549	1,593	190.2%	Kern	25	533	2032.0%
Fresno	590	1,380	133.9%	Fresno	40	402	905.0%
Madera	92	215	133.7%	Madera	6	55	816.7%
Merced	214	642	200.0%	Merced	7	240	3328.6%
Tulare	258	428	65.9%	Tulare	17	142	735.3%
Yolo	77	232	201.3%	Yolo	1	103	10200.0%
El Dorado	86	222	158.1%	El Dorado	4	89	2125.0%
Stanislaus	407	1,286	216.0%	Stanislaus	36	522	1350.0%

CHAPTER 7

The Top Seven Reasons I Like to Buy From the Bank

1. It's a treasure hunt.
2. The dirty work is done.
3. You can negotiate with the bank.
4. The equity is intact.
5. There is great financing and you can close quickly.
6. There will be future deals.
7. The bank's gotta sell.

Working the Bank's Foreclosure Lists Is a Challenging Treasure Hunt

Every lending institution has a list of the properties they are trying to liquidate. You may not find it every time, but it is there. I remember the breathless anticipation I felt in the 1990s when the new lists of VA foreclosures came out every two weeks. My friends used to tell me they couldn't wait for the FHA repo list to

> **DEXTIP**
> Knowing how the numbers tell a story is key. Since the NODs have more than doubled in most counties, this huge jump in non-paying loans will predict the number of houses going to trustee sale. Trustee sales will explode the next time Data Quick publishes these numbers. *We are just getting started!*

come out. For astute real estate investors who knew what they were doing, it was like shooting fish in a barrel!

In the early stages of a down cycle, when banks are not getting as much property back, the inventory list is small. Homeowners can always sell or refi when they get into trouble. But as you get further into a real estate recession, the inventory list grows and the properties stay on the lists longer as they become harder to sell. That is when the real fun starts.

Eleven Reasons the Bank Wants to Sell You the Property NOW

When I see a stagnant REO property that is getting passed over because nobody wants to risk buying it, I know that eleven things are going on:

1. The bank has it priced too high.
2. It may be an expensive property.
3. The property may be in poor condition. Most banks do minimal maintenance until they have a buyer.
4. Carrying costs for the bank are mounting. Bills such as property taxes, water/sewer, insurance, condo homeowner association dues, winterizing and lawn maintenance are just a few of what they have to pay.
5. Banks are feeling increasing pressure from a governmental entity.
6. If the bank has a lot of REOs, it may not be able to borrow money from the Federal Reserve or may have to pay a higher interest rate on the money they borrow from the Fed.
7. You will have a frustrated bank employee in charge of liquidating it.
8. You will have a frustrated Realtor in charge of marketing it. Banks often assume the Realtor will act as general contractor. But most Realtors only sell property; they often don't know much about fixing it up. Often, months go by while the bank and the Realtor go back and forth deciding what to do.
9. It may have slipped through the cracks; sometimes, they forget about it.
10. The property deteriorates over time.
11. The property may be owned by a bank in another state.

What is treasure for us investors and homebuyers is a pain in the neck for the banker until he disposes of it. As you can see, banks operate with a much different set of rules than a private seller. If you know these rules, you will profit.

All the Dirty Work Is Done for You

Buying property that has gone through a foreclosure sale means all junior liens have been wiped out. No judgments, no second mortgages, no mechanic liens and no other funny stuff will appear on the title. The property taxes have been paid and the property is vacant.

> **DEXTIP**
> Solve the bank's problem. Find an REO occupied by a tenant *before* it hits the market. Buy cheap because YOU are going to evict the tenant, saving the bank time and money.

Buying a bank REO is a cleaner transaction than buying directly from a seller who may have a clouded title. Title claims from disaffected spouses, divorces, distant heirs or any other title flaws are generally nullified. You know what you are getting and you also get to inspect property closely to estimate repairs. Property taxes have to be brought current by the lender as well.

The former owner is gone, too. If you ever had to do an eviction, or bought from an owner who didn't leave when he said he would, you know the value of what I say.

Negotiate With the Bank on Fix-up

Regarding the property's general condition, different banks have different ideas about what they will do to a property. What one bank calls a property in marketable condition, another bank will call junk.

Banks are not set up to deal with the renovation of a property. They may end up over-improving a property, but usually get the property painted and that's about it. So REO properties are often dogs.

Therein lays the advantage.

> **DEXTIP**
> Send the asset manager the property's most unflattering picture, one you shot from the worst angle.

I remember when I bought an REO property in Garden Grove, California. It was a real fixer. It needed everything: paint, carpet, flooring and a minor kitchen/bathroom remodel. The bank said to get some contractor estimates for repairs and it would knock them off the price. I tried to have it come off the down payment but the bank wouldn't agree.

We used a property inspector to go over the place with a fine tooth comb. The bank fixed everything, but not at the price we agreed on. That house has been a stellar performer in a Grade A, pride-of-ownership neighborhood. Property rents have increased well over 5% a year in that area.

Intact Equity

This is the best part. When you buy a property below the market value, you have intact equity. Depending on the property you buy, banks can discount on price anywhere from 5% to 35% or more. Intact equity means your properties will cash flow better; it is a buffer against market fluctuations and greatly compounds the returns on your principal.

Instant equity means:

1. **Better cash flow.** Obviously, the less you borrow, the lower your payments are. For example, on a $400,000 loan, your payments at 7% interest will be $2,661 a month. If you buy that same house at a 12% discount and you borrowed only $350,000, your loan payment would be $331 less or only be $2,328 a month, making for a 12% discount.

    > **DEXTIP**
    > Astute real estate investors never pay retail for anything.

    Rents do not have to rise as much to make negative cash flow property break even, and it is easier to qualify for a loan.

2. **Buffer against market fluctuations**. If house prices in the area where you buy go down further, intact equity can mean the difference between a short sale, a foreclosure, or not losing any money at all.

    If you do not think that is important, I would remind you about all the beginning investors who paid retail for their properties, which are now feeding the foreclosure markets.

3. **Intact equity supercharges returns on your capital.** That portion for which you bought the property below market has a return on it. For example, if you bought a house for $400,000 and years later it appreciated to $500,000, the return on your $400,000 investment would be $100,000, or 25%. However, if you got a 13% discount off market value from the bank and only paid $350,000 for that same house that went up in value to $500,000,

the return is now 43%. Better yet, that intact equity of $50,000 has a return on it as well. *The yield on your $50,000 is 300%!*

Can you see why astute real estate investors seldom pay retail for anything?

Get Great Financing and Close Quickly

Not all banks will do this, but they will often give you a great loan on the property on which they just foreclosed. Lenders' REO departments have a special relationship with their lending division and will offer *expedited financing.*

One REO I bought in Corona, CA, came with a 10% down, Eleventh District Cost of Funds adjustable rate loan. They rushed that loan through in seven days with little cost. We closed the day after Christmas so they got that non-performing asset off their books before year end. At that time my credit scores were lower, my income was undocumentable and I had a lot of properties showing up on my credit report. But they rushed that loan straight through and called me a "seasoned investor."

That was not a bad loan to start off with, but it gets better. Several years later, they offered me a fixed rate at 5.7%, which I gladly took. That property is a great positive cash flowing asset today and has tripled in value.

Once you get the bank in escrow, don't expect many delays. They are in the business to liquidate.

It's Great to Know the Asset Mangers/Realtor/Brokers Who Are Unemotional and Businesslike

You can deal with these players for future deals. If you work the REO market, getting to know these people who are getting all these distressed deals is time very well spent.

To these guys, the house is just an asset that needs to be disposed of. It's all numbers to them. The manager of an REO department or an asset manager who is dealing with hedge fund investors operates in a different universe than an emotional seller who is selling the family castle.

I will go into detail about these players later but, if you come off like a pro, they will deal with you first. Since I have bought houses from them, they always take my calls because I am brief, to the point and do not waste their time. Plus, I always tell them what their counterparts at other REO departments are up to.

Find Them in Great Neighborhoods

There is great benefit in finding properties in prime neighborhoods. When a real estate market begins to pull back during recessionary times, the first properties that show up on lenders' REO lists are:

1. Condos
2. Remote properties far from the job base
3. Houses in primarily renter-occupied areas
4. Properties with material defects (the odd houses, nonconforming to the neighborhood, on busy streets, next to railroad tracks, adjacent to commercial areas)
5. Outdated houses
6. Odd configurations
7. Old, turn-of-the-century houses
8. Nicer houses in good neighborhoods

> **DEXTIP**
> Be polite, patient and persistent to nurture your source of future deals. It's all about building relationships.

I like the nicer neighborhoods. Higher quality properties come last because they are more desirable, and the wealthier homeowners generally have more staying power to weather downturns. Depending on the attractiveness and desirability of these properties, they can fly off these REO lists faster and for more money. But they do show up, and in great numbers.

However, high-end properties can sell for far greater discounts because there is higher variability at that price level, there is a smaller buyer population and the bank has more money tied up in it.

If you are going to be a buy and hold investor, having houses in quality neighborhoods dramatically makes property management easier and the real estate in those areas appreciates more.

Astute real estate investors are always trying to upgrade their portfolio of houses to one of higher quality and more worth. When you buy quality houses that come onto the market at greater discount, you maximize your returns and minimize your hassle.

Banks Want and Need to Sell Their REO Inventory

Of course, banks are motivated to get non-performing assets off of their books. Good asset managers are leaning on their agents to get the property fixed up and ready for market, and yelling at them when it doesn't sell. It does not look good to have a whole bunch of declining-in-value inventory sitting on the bank's balance sheet.

At the same time, those managers are getting pressure from above. Even though no seller wants to let a property go for a song, harried REO managers feel pressure from:

1. The bank's stockholders, who want profit;
2. The hedge fund investors, who want their money back;
3. The bank's board of directors, who want the government regulators out of their hair; the more dead assets (REOs) the bank carries, the less money they can lend out and the more the Federal Reserve raises their interest costs.
4. The immediate boss, who is wondering why that asset manager's inventory is not moving.

Knowing this, the astute investor is never disrespectful to the bank managers, asset managers and bank Realtors who are up against it. Everybody knows they have to unload their repossessed property, and they know it, too. All bank managers, or their representatives, tell me they hate dealing with rude, ignorant and beginning investors who just came from their first REO seminar expecting to buy property for half price.

You shouldn't be one of those ignoramuses, either.

Conclusion

Knowing where all these foreclosures are coming from, who's got them and how much longer it is likely to last is a great background for knowing how to proceed in this booming REO market.

We are now in the part of the price cycle where the lenders have the foreclosure deals. Post-foreclosures are where the action will be for years, so as we go deeper into this soft market, be ready for the REO managers to deal. The astute real estate investor takes advantage of economic trends and strikes when bargains abound. Now, let's talk about how to get them!

CHAPTER 8

Who's Got the Bargains, How to Find Them, Where They Are, Who to Talk to and What to Do Next

This is probably one of the most important chapters you will ever read. We have already learned why this trend in bank REOs is here, how long it is likely to last and in what regions of the United States these properties are most likely to be found due to the subprime meltdown. Now, we will:

1. See which banks have the most REOS;
2. Uncover ten ways to find the people to talk to;
3. Learn how to negotiate the best price;
4. See whether it the best investment for you;
5. See which REOs I like and which I don't like;
6. Identify areas and properties to avoid;
7. Discover what to hold for long-term appreciation or to flip for quick cash;
8. Show ways to deal with and overcome negative cash flow;
9. Find out how to make your best offer;
10. Be able to tell what your property will be worth five, ten or twenty years from now;
11. Examine how to flip property;
12. Understand that it will get better.

Who's Got Them and Who's Got the Most
Courtesy of www.all-foreclosure.com (California only)

Bank	4-20-07	11-15-08	% Increase
Freddie Mac	66	3077	4662%
Horizon	240	945	394%
REO Source	142	2967	2089%
B of A	13	546	4200%
Countrywide	1208	5965	494%
Downey	45	561	1147%
Indy Mac	52	1032	1882%
Ocwen	301	889	195%
Wells Fargo	1780	5035	283%
Wachovia	23	765	3220%

DEXTIP
There are a lot more REOs out there; this list is not exhaustive. Hedge funds and Wall Street mortgage bankers do not show up here and not all banks update their listings. Use these banks as a starting point to establish your relationships. Go to *www.all-foreclosure.com* to find them.

Ten Ways to Find out Who to Talk to (The Bank's REO Manager)

Any lender who loans money for the purchase or refinancing of real estate will have to foreclose at some point soon. This could even be you, if you were a private lender or did hard money loans. Then for that foreclosed property, you would be your own REO manager. REO managers have to:

1. Start foreclosure proceedings and not violate state and federal laws;
2. If you are in one of the thirty-four states that foreclose by trust deed, get a trustee to handle the foreclosure from the initial notice of default until after the property's sale at the courthouse steps.

3. If it is a mortgage state, you must do a judicial foreclosure. To get the property reverted, you must hire an attorney, file a lawsuit and go to court.
4. Try to find a real estate agent who knows what he or she is doing: managing the asset, marketing the property to your satisfaction and keeping you updated.
5. Evict the tenant or former owner.
6. Get the property fixed up well enough to sell.
7. Put the property on the MLS and get it sold.
8. Negotiate with buyers who don't qualify and fall out of escrow.
9. Get the highest price you can.

With banks, it is the same job as with any private seller, but the work is multiplied. Over the last several years, I have kept in touch with several bank REO managers, and they have become my friends. When the market is good (houses are appreciating, sales are up and inventory is down because properties are selling quickly), the bank's REO staff has little to do. They get laid off or reassigned to other duties within the bank.

But when the market slows down and foreclosures mount, REO mangers must:

1. Deal with exploding inventory—they may have hundreds, perhaps thousands, of properties to look after;
2. If property is owned by investors, track them down for purchase and pricing decisions;
3. Hire new staff and bring them up to speed;
4. Keep on top of increasing piles of paperwork;
5. Contact all the different cities to keep the utilities on;
6. Write checks to contractors;
7. Deal with bad agents who bring them:
    a. Bad advice and overpriced BPOs (broker's price opinions);
    b. Unqualified buyers;
    c. Trivial excuses why things do not get done;
8. Hope the escrow closes;
9. Sell the property, get the check, close the file.

You need to know where the banks' REO managers are coming from. The more you know about their job, the more they will want to deal with you. Keep this in mind when we talk about how to negotiate with the banks in later chapters.

Contacting the Bank's REO Department

If you were to walk into the local branch of your bank and ask where the REO department is, most likely you would be met with a blank stare. I have even had them say, "Oh, we don't have those OREOS. You have to go to the grocery store to get Oreos."

But they do have them, and in abundant supply. Every lender who puts a lien on property will end up having to seize the collateral sometimes. Big banks have entire staffs dedicated to liquidating repossessed inventory. How do we find the person in charge, the one who can make a deal, and the one person we can get on the phone who can accept or decline our offer?

Ten of the Best Ways to Find Bank Foreclosures Within an Hour's Drive of Your Home

It ain't easy and it requires some detective work, but I have some ideas for you:

1. Foreclosure trustees
2. Make a direct offer after the trustee sale.
3. Online foreclosure tracking services
4. Asset manager conventions (hobnob around and buy drinks)
5. Networking
6. Get to know people who work at banks and have them nose around the foreclosure departments.
7. Your real estate agent
8. Newspapers and other publications
9. Ride the Internet.
10. Attend auctions.

I'll tell you how I did it. After months of fruitlessly pounding on the doors of homeowners in foreclosure, I started calling the trustees handling the sale. Most of the time, I just got a recorded message; other times I met with some resistance trying to get internal phone numbers for the bank. Then I started calling the beneficiaries listed on the report, with much of the same result. In the trustee state of California, the listed beneficiary is also the lender. The trustee is usually an attorney or a foreclosure service that handles the sale.

Call the Foreclosure Trustees or the Foreclosing Attorney

The addresses of the beneficiaries were also listed, so I did a reverse address search to look for a good phone number…with limited results. I questioned the trustees about how I should go about it, and they suggested I keep trying because I was on the right track. Finally, one trustee said, "Oh, you need to talk to Doris at the bank. She will help you. Would you like her phone number?" **"Yes, I would**!"

Doris and I closed two weeks later on a property bought at 20% below market value.

Below is an actual public notice of sale for a property that was going to auction at 10 A.M. on the courthouse steps on July 27, 2007. In **bold** is an example of the numbers that I was calling in my strenuous efforts to find the bank's decision maker. In **bold** is the pertinent info.

Subject & Owner: Joe Homeowner
Parcel: 93987552
County: OR
Page/Grid: 921/C5
Site Address: 1 Alberta Aliso Viejo, CA 92656-6058
Mail Address: 1 Alberta Aliso Viejo, CA 92656-6058

Trustee & Lender
Trustee: Alliance Title Co.
4665 Macarthur Ct.
Newport Beach, CA 92660
(949) 252-2800 Ext#

Lender: Fremont Invs & Ln
4665 Macarthur Ct.
Newport Beach, CA 92660
(949) 252-2800 Ext#

Default Information NOD Doc #: 0000218873 Rec. Date: 04/04/2007
Delq. Amt: $13,413 as of: 04/03/2007
Loan #: 0000727143
Default Date: 09/14/2005
Loan Amt: $479,200
Principal: $479,200
Trustee Sale
Sale # 07-7094-CA-M
Auct. Date: 07/27/2007: 10:00 AM

Auct. Loc: 401 E Chapman Ave.
Placentia
Bid: $492,088
NOT Doc #: 0000433148
Rec. Date: 07/11/2007
Loan #: 0000727143
**Property & Sale Sq Ft: 1,363 Yr Blt: 1996 Lot Size: Bdrm: 3 Garage:
G 2 Bath: 2.50**
Zone: Units: 1

To summarize: Here we have Joe Homeowner losing his Aliso Viejo, 3-bedroom, 2.5-bathroom, 1,363-square foot house to a foreclosure sale on July 27, 2007, at ten o'clock in the morning on the courthouse steps. The foreclosure trustee, Alliance Title, is handling the sale for its client-beneficiary, Fremont Investment and Loan, and recorded the notice of trustee sale on July 11, 2007. This property is guaranteed to go back to the bank because the default amount is not much over market value. It is upside down.

If I liked this property, I would call the trustee, Alliance Title Co., to find a better phone number for the beneficiary, Fremont Investment and Loan. I would also call Fremont, the beneficiary, who is also the foreclosing lender, to locate the decision maker.

Following the Property Past the Sale and Finding REOs Ahead of the Pack

If I REALLY liked the property, I would do a preliminary strike. When I was sure that the property was going to revert to that address of the beneficiary, I would send an offer with a sizable cashier's check directly to the REO manager. That check, along with some unflattering photos of the property, would absolutely get their attention.

> **DEXTIP**
> Be proactive and creative. Follow a property when it reverts back to the bank immediately after the foreclosure sale. Federal Express an offer to the bank's president with no conditions and a sizable cashier's check to get their attention. Ugly photos of the property help.

Foreclosure Tracking Services

Foreclosures are public information and usually show up in a legal newspaper in your town. Where I live, it is called the *Daily Commerce*. It is much easier to use a paid foreclosure tracking service, such as:

1. www.realtytrac.com
2. www.foreclosures.com
3. www.countyrecordsresearch.com

They are much easier to use and will often give you sales comparables of surrounding property. Or you can try getting sales comparables for free from a local title company.

Asset Manager Conventions

Go where they go, read what they read. If you can establish just one contact at these conventions that meet several times a year, it could be worth millions. They get back scads of property, like right now. They are probably pretty stressed out and hiding under the table in advance of the coming tidal wave. In other words, they don't want to talk to you.

You may have to sneak in or join their organization as an affiliate but it would be worth it. To find out where they meet, read what asset managers read:

1. www.reonationwide.com
2. www.reomac.com
3. www.reomanager.com
4. www.reobroker.com
5. www.reoworld.com

Networking and Getting to Know the People Who Work at the Banks

Another REO asset manager I found worked at Countrywide. She was presenting at an REOMAC convention, giving tips on how to become a bank broker. She lets me know trends at Countrywide and what properties she has coming down the track. I have not yet bought an REO from her, but I probably will at some point.

One former loan agent I got to know went to work for a bank's asset management department. He let me know properties the bank was getting back before they hit the listing books. I can't say I bought any houses from this contact, but if I find the right house in a neighborhood I like at a good price, I will buy.

Your Real Estate Agent

Have your real estate agent find REOs on the MLS. Once your agent knows what to look for, you can have her find REOs and you can pick and choose the ones that have the most potential. It will not take your agent much time to find REOs if she knows what to look for.

First, ask your real estate agent to go into the multiple listing service and find all of the foreclosure properties that are listed. The multiple listing service, also known as the MLS, is a computerized service that provides real estate agents with a detailed and comprehensive list of all the properties that are currently on the market and available for purchase. The MLS is available throughout the U.S. It contains thousands and thousands of listings. A "listing" is a term real estate agents use to describe a property that they currently have for sale on the real estate market.

Keywords are important. Your agent will have to enter the word as a key search word in the computer. Input keywords into the MLS, such as:

1. REO
2. Bank owned
3. Foreclosure
4. Bank foreclosure
5. Bank repo

Other keywords that will produce MLS hits for distressed property are:

1. Handyman special
2. Fixer
3. Reduced price
4. As is
5. Must relocate
6. Priced under market
7. Instant equity
8. Owner will carry
9. A steal
10. Bring all offers
11. Lease option
12. Short Sale
13. Going to auction
14. Distress sale

15. Pre-foreclosure
16. No qualifying
17. Must sell
18. Seller anxious
19. Investor special
20. Corporate owned

These are all the keywords I can think of; perhaps you and your agent could think of some more.

When your agent pulls up all of the foreclosures in the MLS, the owner will be listed as a bank. Many agents do not know this. Make your real estate agent aware of what you are looking for.

Depending upon the size of the town you live in, your agent should come up with an extensive list of REOs. Once your agent has a list of available REOs, ask her to give you the listing summary for each one. A listing summary is a one-page document that the MLS provides to real estate agents for each of the properties in its directory. It gives detailed information about each property. Here is the information you will look for in the listing summary:

- The property's address
- The asking price
- The type of property: single family home, townhouse or condominium
- The number of bedrooms and bathrooms
- The number of days that the property has been on the market. This is important because the longer the property sits unsold, the more anxious the bank will be to get rid of it. Make offers on properties that have been on the market the longest period of time.
- Give priority to properties that are in poor condition. A brief description of the property will include its current condition and any other important facts. There is a lot of information on the listing summary and there is not much room for a description. It may be just two of three brief sentences. Pay particularly close attention to the description.

Beat the Banks

> **DEXTIP**
> Properties that are just sitting, doing nothing for long periods of time and properties in bad condition are a real nightmare for banks. Banks are very motivated to sell them — at a loss.

Sit down with your real estate agent and have her show you how to read a listing summary. It should only take a few minutes. Listing summaries are very easy to read once you know what to look for.

Finally, have your real estate agent call the listing agent. The listing agent is the real estate agent who was hired by the bank to sell the REO. Have your agent ask the bank's agent if there have been any offers.

You may discover that there have been two or three offers on the property that have been turned down by the bank. This is a sure sign that you are dealing with an unmotivated bank, but that can quickly change because:

1. A new asset manager gets assigned to the property;
2. Paperwork piles on their desk gets larger;
3. Management gives the word to dump.

Next, have your agent try to find out the amount of money that was offered. Some agents will furnish this information and some will not. The listing agent (who works for the bank) is not obligated to give your agent this information. If your agent finds that the rejected offers were higher than yours will be, then you should move on to another REO.

As with all foreclosure investing, you want to spend a limited amount of time and effort on each prospect. Do not waste a lot of time on any one property. Of course, once you have one in your sights, you should take as much time as needed to make sure the property is sold to you for the lowest price you can get for it.

I have pulled an actual bank listing from the multiple listing service and have put the information that you should pay attention to in **bold**.

Residential
Single Family Residence
Detached RES Active *1401 W Dogwood Ave* Anaheim **(ANA)**   **Price $504,900***

Anaheim East of Harbor (78)	Zip 92801-3615	TGNO *768F3*
Orange County (OR)	XSTS Euclid & La Palma Aerial Map	
P583047	*Media: 12*	Builder Tract Other (OTHR)
Bed 4	Model (0)	**Baths 2** Style Other

Stories One Level	Floor	
HOA Dues $ 0 + $	$	
SqFt 1,325	**Assessor**	**YrBlt 1955**
Assessor	Land Fee	LotSize 7,260 Assessor D i m
Acres 0.17		

Prkng Direct Garage Access, Garage Attached
Garage 2 A

** **Bank Owned** ** **Reduced $50K for a quick sale!!** Charming home on a nice, quiet street. Plenty of upgrades. Completely remodeled kitchen & renovated bathrooms w/new tile decor. Cozy hardwood floor thru out. Perfect for homecare use! All 4 bedrooms have outside access, wheelchair access & individual locks. Remodeled cabinets, window & garage. Large yard with surrounding fence & gate for safety. Easy access to hwys & shopping.

Rooms

Bedrooms All Bedrooms Down, Ground Floor Master Bedroom, Main Floor Bedroom, Main Floor Master Bedroom, Living Rm Living Rm Entrance, Living Room   Dining In Kitchen, Other Laundry In Garage

Amenities

Pool No Pool, Spa No Spa, TV Cable TV, Firepl Living Room, Security, Appliances Built-In Gas Range, Convection Oven, Dishwasher, Gas/Elec Dryer Hook Up, Other , High or Mid-Rise Amenities

Interior

Heating Forced Air, Cooling Attic Fan, Floors Hardwood, Interior Misc

Exterior/Structural

Entry Location Ground Level - no steps , Common Walls, Roof Composition/Shingle, Plumbing , Patio Patio, Cond , Sprinklers Front, Side and Rear , Doors/Windows, Exterior Construction Stucco

Lot Description

APNO 034-421-02 , Zoning , Lot/Block/Tract 83//2161, Lot , Legal, Sewer In, Connected & Paid, Water District, Yard, Community/Association, HS Dist Anaheim Union High School District, Elemen , Junior , High Sch, Amenities, Units, HOA Dues $ 0+ $, Mello Roos No, Land Fee, Lse Trans $, Land Lse/Yr $, Lse Ren , Lse Exp, City Inspect No, Builder's Name

Listing Activity

List Date 6/12/2007	**Date Added 6/12/2007**	**Tran Date 7/23/2007**
LP/SqFt $381.06		
Org Price $ 529,900	**Prev Price $ 514,900**	**Cur List Prc $504,900**

To summarize, this four-bedroom/two-bathroom single family residence (SFR), built in 1955, was listed one month ago for $529,900. One month later the price of this 1,325-square foot SFR was $504,900.

I like the neighborhood and it is the right size for a good rental house. I don't like the fact that it is a four-bedroom since it will attract tenants with daycares, board and cares, foster homes, home cares for the old and disabled, special needs kids or large blended families with many adults. All of this translates into heavy wear on the house. But I am willing to deal with those management issues since it is a pride-of-ownership neighborhood.

Is $504,900 the right price? Let's take a look at the comps:

Comparable Sales Data

No.	Address	Date	Price	$/SF	Bld/Area	RM/BR/Bth	YB	Lot Area	Pool	Proxim.
	Subject Property	03/15/2007	$505,814	$385	1,313	/4/2.0	1955	7,260 SF		
1	1507 W CATHERINE DR	06/18/2007	$550,000	$419	1313	7/4/2.0	1955	6,000 SF		.11Mi.
2	1033 N HERMOSA DR	05/01/2007	$704,000	$375	1875	7/3/2.0	1954	6,656 SF		.10Mi.
3	1517 W FRANCES DR	12/19/2006	$585,000	$446	1312	7/4/2.0	1955	6,000 SF		.08Mi.
4	1306 W IONIA PL	10/05/2006	$635,500	$495	1285	7/4/2.0	1955	6,305 SF		.24Mi.

All the comps are close by and of similar size. It looks like comp #1 is a model match but the sale is two months old; comp #2 is priced way out of market and comps #3 and #4 are too old to bother with.

Given the condition of this REO, the bank (Bank of New York) is dreaming. Fixed up in perfect condition, it may well be $50,000 below market, which is a 10% discount, but the comps are going for less and less every day. Because of this market volatility, I'd *have to* have a very healthy buffer. If I wanted it, I would offer $375,000 and settle on $400,000 if they did the financing and paid closing costs. If they did not like the offer, I would go on to the next one.

If I had gotten it for $375,000, that would be 68% of the original list price. Does that mean I got it for sixty-eight cents on the dollar? What do you think?

UPDATE!!

I wrote the above words in the summer of 2007. How have the prices fared since then? Let's take a look at the prices as of spring 2008 to see how that Anaheim, CA, neighborhood has gone down in price.

☑ 1	1418 W FRANCES DR, 92801-3639	0.09	3	2.00	1,053	6,000	1955	**02/13/2008**	**$380,000**	$360.87
☑ 2	929 N MOHICAN AVE, 92801-3512	0.40	3	2.00	1,148	6,695	1955	**01/04/2008**	**$419,000**	$364.98
☑ 3	1305 N CONDOR ST, 92801-2153	0.50	3	1.00	1,320	6,240	1957	**11/16/2007**	**$400,000**	$303.03
☑ 4	460 W ROBERTA AVE 92832-3233	0.72	4	2.00	1,741	6,700	1958	**10/31/2007**	**$448,000**	$257.32
☑ 5	1513 S CITRUS AVE, 92833-4727	0.74	3	2.00	1,495	7,210	1958	**11/16/2007**	**$555,000**	$371.24
☑ 6	1205 W CONNECTICUT AVE, 92801-5910	0.75	3	1.00	2,011	9,350	1958	**10/26/2007**	**$590,000**	$293.39

Hmm... Not many sales, and each house sells for less as time goes by. Looks like that $375,000 wholesale price I would have paid in June 2007 is now close to retail market value. The lowest comps put today's price at $380,000 to $400,000, not much more.Interesting. Bank of New York tried to sell it for $504,900 in June 2007, and it was worth close to $380,000 to $400,000 as of February 2008. Does that mean prices have declined 20% in nine months? Annualized, that decline is 26% a year.

Does that mean that the same house will go for a retail price of $300,000 in a year's time? Perhaps.

Read the Newspapers

"How do you find those bank foreclosures? How do I do it like you do?" I hear that all the time. I bought a bank REO by simply contacting the asset manager listed in the newspaper, and I got it for eighty cents on the dollar.

The local throwaway paper (*Pennysaver*, *The Nickel*) or community papers can be excellent ways to find Realtors who have distressed listings. Here are two of the popular websites to look at for distressed listings and to establish relationships with the agents who get them:

1. www.pennysaverusa.com
2. www.greenandwhitesheets.com

Ride the Internet for Free Bank Websites

This was not here the last time around. I would have loved to have the ability to surf over fifty bank REO websites for foreclosures all across the country. Now you can. **Go to *www.all-foreclosure.com* (*http://www.all-foreclosure.com/fore-closures.htm*) for the mother of all REO websites.**

Foreclosures from government agencies are in the first section, including property owned by HUD, VA, Fannie Mae and Freddie Mac. The second section includes property listed by asset managers, who will usually have foreclosures listed from different lenders. The third section contains listings provided directly by banks or institutions owning the property; these lists are often limited by region. If you are interested in a specific region, check that third section for a regional bank. You'll find by looking at the individual links that most foreclosed homes are going to be listed by perhaps ten of the sources, including Fannie Mae, Homesteps, HUD, VA, Countrywide and a couple of the larger asset managers. Here is a sampling of what you will find there:

> **DEXTIP**
> Throwaway papers are magnets for bottom-fishing agents trolling for customers.

GOVERNMENT HOME SALES A site containing predominately VA and HUD foreclosed properties; submitting an offer requires the use of a real estate agent.

HUD FORECLOSURES It's probably easier to use the government home sales link above rather than working through the various HUD pages.

FANNIE MAE FORECLOSURE LISTINGS They buy loans on the secondary market; if the property is foreclosed, Fannie Mae will end up being the owner of the real estate. Searchable by city, state and ZIP code.

FREDDIE MAC (HOMESTEPS) Database searchable by features, including city, state, zip code, county, bedrooms and bathrooms. Similar to Fannie Mae, it is a purchaser of loans on the secondary market.

Government Foreclosures

VA Use the government home sales site above.

FEDERAL DEPOSIT INSURANCE CORPORATION (GOVERNMENT) National list, but not many properties

SMALL BUSINESS ADMINISTRATION (GOVERNMENT) Real estate throughout the U.S.

UNITED STATES DEPARTMENT OF AGRICULTURE You can search for single-family, farms or multi-family property.

KENTUCKY HOUSING CORPORATION Limited properties in Kentucky

Asset Manager Foreclosures

FIRST PRESTON First Preston manages and markets HUD property in Georgia, Kansas, Kentucky, Missouri, Oklahoma, Tennessee and Texas.

HMB, INC. HMB manages and markets HUD properties in Alaska, Idaho, Illinois, Indiana, North Carolina, Oregon, South Carolina, Virginia, Washington and West Virginia.

HORIZON MANAGEMENT SERVICES National database; select by state. (Contributed by Becky.)

INTEGRATED ASSET SERVICES Foreclosure homes in Alabama, Arkansas, Colorado, Delaware, Florida, Georgia, Iowa, Idaho, Illinois, Indiana, Kansas, Kentucky, Louisiana, Massachusetts, Maryland, Michigan, Minnesota and Missouri

KEYSTONE ASSET MANAGEMENT Foreclosed homes in Alabama, Georgia, New York, Ohio and Pennsylvania. Other states are also available; just search for the state you'd like.

LENDERS ASSET MANAGEMENT CORP. Various states; search for the ones that interest you.

REO SOURCE Nationwide; search by state or zip code.

MLNUSA Properties throughout the U.S. Use the map to search by state. (Contributed by Sal.)

PREMIERE ASSET SERVICES National search

TREO Listings throughout the U.S. Use the properties link on the left side.

REO NATIONWIDE
Nationwide long list, not a database, so it takes a while to load (REOWORLD.COM).

Bank Foreclosures

AMERICA TAX FUNDING Not really a bank, they have tax certificate foreclosed property. (Contributed by Sal.)

NATIONAL BANK OF ARIZONA Owned by National Bank of Arizona

BANK OF AMERICA FORECLOSURES One of the largest lenders in the U.S.; you can search for residential or commercial.

BEAL BANK Beal commercial properties

BRANCH BANKING & TRUST Searchable list of states

CITIMORTGAGE REO Search by state or property type. (Contributed by Sal.)

COMPASS BANK Foreclosed property listed mostly in Alabama and Texas, some in New Mexico and Colorado

COUNTRYWIDE FORECLOSURES The largest independent home loan originator, they have property thoughout the United States.

DOWNEY SAVINGS & LOAN Downey Savings is regional, so you will find homes listed in the Western United States.

FREMONT INVESTMENT & LOAN Small selection of properties from an independent lender

FORECLOSURENET National coverage; fee for service with a FREE seven-day trial

GMAC COMMERCIAL MORTGAGE Commercial properties throughout the U.S.

GRP FINANCIAL SERVICES

HOME LOAN BANK Wisconsin, Michigan, Pennsylvania, New York, Maine and Texas

HSBC PRIVATE BANK Georgia, Missouri, New York, Ohio, South Carolina and Texas

INDYMAC Many states listed; they also have a lot of manufactured housing listed.

LEXINGTON STATE BANK Small list of North Carolina properties

MANUFACTURERS & TRADERS TRUST Huge amounts of property available

MIDLAND MORTGAGE Map search or search by state. (Contributed by Sal.)

NEW SOUTH FEDERAL BANK Alabama, Louisiana and Tennessee`

OCWEN Large buyer/servicer of non-performing loans

PEOPLES BANK Predominantly has homes in Connecticut.

TEXAS STATE BANK Commercial, residential and land listings

UNITY BANK New Jersey properties

U.S. BANK HOME MORTGAGE Throughout the U.S.

VIRGINIA HOUSING DEVELOPMENT Property in Virginia

Attend Bank Auctions

It is happening again. In the last real estate downturn, banks were so flooded with foreclosures that they resorted to auctioneers who would sell off their repossessed inventory. Liquidation auctions by the FDIC and the RTC during the late 1980s' thrift and loan crisis were common, and astute investors profited greatly.

Banks, asset managers and other agencies find it convenient to gather all buyers in a large meeting hall, hire an auction company and sell to the highest bidder. Auctions are of two types: absolute auctions and reserve auctions. Absolute auctions mean the property will be sold, no matter how low the bid. That property will be sold to someone that day.

Reserve auctions mean the bank has a minimum price in mind, but they do not tell anybody what that reserve amount is. They usually list what the last sale price was and perhaps a starting or minimum bid. It's like giving you the low range and the high range in price of what they expect, but they are under no obligation to sell.

> **DEXTIP**
> Opportunities are to be had by going to bank liquidation auctions. Do your homework first. Deals at future bank auctions should be massive!

> **DEXTIP**
> Bank auction websites will be extremely busy for the foreseeable future. Mine them.

Here are the eight auction companies that banks most often use:

1. Real Estate Disposition Corp. (REDC) *www.ushomeauction.com*
2. Kennedy Wilson *http://www.kwiauctions.com*
3. Hudson and Marshall *http://www.hudsonandmarshall.com*
4. Williams and Williams *http://www.williamsauction.com/Home.aspx*
5. Premier Estates *http://www.premiereestates.com/*
6. Quick REO Capital *www.quickreo.com*
7. National Home Auction Corp. *www.homeauctiondirect.com*
8. Catalist Homes *www.catalisthomes.com*

Below are some websites that some REO property has shown up on. Take a look, but I cannot vouch for them:

1. JP King *http://www.jpking.com/*
2. Surf and Country Real Estate
   http://www.surfandcountry.com/auctions.php
3. Realty Bid *http://www.realtybid.com/*
4. Bear Stearns Asset Management Services *http://www.stearnsassetservices.com/*
5. *www.buybankhomes.com* The auctioneer makes his money by charging a 5%-10% buyer's premium that you pay.

Are these good deals? I've heard mixed results, but I am sure timing will be key. With barrels of houses coming back to the bank, bargains will abound at future auctions.

Bank Auctions Are a Lot of Work

Working the REO auctions is a lot of work, especially the big ones that have a lot of property, because:

1. Hordes of investors and gawkers crowd mammoth convention halls, thereby increasing competition.
2. The sheer volume of inventory.

Bargains are to be found in these auctions, but you will have to persevere. Auction companies work for the bank so they want to bring in as many prospective buyers as possible. Consequently, homes can get bid on close to retail prices in these loud, cacophonous meeting spaces—not what you are looking for.

> **DEXTIP**
> On all of these bank auction websites, you can register to get notified by e-mail of their impending auctions. The smaller auction companies are not as well publicized so they are not so well attended.

Open houses are held before the auction weekend. Drive and inspect as many as you can. You have to look at a lot of homes to find the ones that are priced where you want them. It is best to have specific criteria.

The bidding is quick and final. Be on the alert, or you may lose out on your property. Most successful bidders arrive at the auction hall **very well prepared.** Have your maximum bid amount already established so you don't get caught up in the excitement. You will forget what you are bidding on so have a notebook at the ready with every property's data in one place. This notebook should contain:

1. The bid number or the auction ID number of the property
2. Pictures
3. Inspection list of defects
4. Sales comparables of surrounding sales and listing prices
5. Personal comments about the condition
6. Maximum bid amount

Don't deviate from your maximum bid price. You won't lose out because there are many more bank foreclosure auctions coming. It's like sitting on a bus bench: the bus comes, some people get on and some get off, but there is always another bus coming.

If you are going to flip your new purchase, you better know very well what your thirty-day sales price is.

The Five Biggest Mistakes Bidders Make at REO Auctions

1. Underestimating how long it takes for a quick resale
2. Underestimating cost of repairs
3. Don't fix it all the way up for a retail sale
4. Buying in marginal neighborhoods
5. Buying in areas of low sales activity
6. Overpaying

CHAPTER 9

Negotiating With the Bank

Banks often market their listings directly to the consumer, although most are hesitant to do this and will instead use a Realtor. They will tell you to call the Realtor who is listing the property because they:

1. Want to get you out of their hair;
2. Do not have the time or ability to handle the volume of calls they get;
3. Feel that a Realtor will better fulfill the legal disclosure requirements of a real estate transaction;
4. Put the Realtor to work because they are paying them for:
   a. Marketing the property;
   b. Making sure the property is maintained and shows well;
   c. Presenting the offer to the bank;
   d. Showing the property;
   e. Managing the property and evicting tenants;
   f. Screening out non-serious buyers;
   g. Regularly reporting back to the bank about the property's status;
   h. Getting the best price;
   i. Opening escrow and closing the sale.

Realtors who work for banks have a lot more to do than just regular agents. Most of the time, they make a smaller commission but then make it up on volume. We will talk about how to deal with bank brokers later.

The bank's asset managers have a tough job to do; they may seem harried and rude. You must understand that they are not there to make your life easy and send you lists of properties for sale. They work on deadline in one of the most chaotic departments in the bank because they get tons of property back fast and every property is a moving target. They are also in charge of getting the bank's money back (at least some of it).

> **DEXTIP**
> Point out that properties are selling slowly. Offer odd numbers; it sounds like you have done your homework. If no deal, thank him and leave your phone number.
> Keep a list of follow-ups.

Make things easy for them, and it will be easier for them to say yes to your offer. Some may not appreciate your polite but firm attitude; most will. You will stand out from most of the buyers they get who are rude, obvious chiselers or newbies just out of their first foreclosure seminar who think banks are having a half-price sale. All bankers negotiate differently:

- With those managers who have large egos, be humble and firm.
- Be persistent with those who are distant and aloof.

In all cases, do your homework. Mention lists of major repairs and point out that there are many other minor repairs to do to bring the property up to saleable standards, even if you are only going to rent it out (for which you do not need to do as much fix-up). Have your list of repairs ready and be accurate. Asset managers love licensed contractors' estimates.

Solve their problems for them and you will have better luck when you negotiate on:

1. Fix-up expenses
2. Evictions
3. Cash
4. Financing

Repairs

When a property becomes an REO, most likely it is not in the greatest condition. Neglect and damage caused by the outgoing owner are very common. Some banks will fix a property all the way up, but most won't. It is good to find a foreclosure in bad shape. *It is better to impress the bank with that fact.*

A good, *ugly* house in a great neighborhood is "pay dirt" because fix-up expenses come off the price and, even better, perhaps off of the down payment. Why? Because you can fix up a house much more cheaply than the bank can. On one deal, I got a contractor to give me a price to fix up the property to saleable condition. We told the bank we wanted to bring it up to saleable condition, but we ended up renting it out so we didn't have to put all that money into it. We saved many thousands of dollars.

> **DEXTIP**
> We found an inexpensive handyman and his crew by going to one of the national handyman chains and offering them side work. He was very good and very cheap.

Out-of-town lenders are up against it. If foreclosing lenders are located out of state, they will not be familiar with the local costs of materials and labor. It is a weak position for the bank to be in, and you can use that to your advantage.

Evictions

Save the bank from this problem and save yourself money. If you have landlord experience, you can save the bank a bundle of money and lots of time by buying the property as is. Tell the bank you will handle the eviction and all the repairs. There will be no inspections and no prolonged escrows. Of course, all these savings will be reflected in a reduced price.

If you are going to be handling the eviction, make sure you know your state's laws. Tenants often leave if you give them a little cash; they know their time is up.

One house I bought had a granddaughter living in it with her drug addict boyfriend. The grandmother/owner did not want to evict her granddaughter and cause waves. So she sold me the house for a cheap price and I evicted the granddaughter. Actually, all I had to do was give them a little bit of cash and they left in a week.

Cash and Volume Discounts

If you have cash, the banks will open the vaults. All sellers like big down payments, and you will get an adjustment on price. All cash deals get the biggest discounts.

Even better, use your cash to buy several properties from the bank. If you offer relief to beleaguered asset managers by getting several properties off their books, they will be eternally grateful.

Every asset manager's inventory includes some doggy property. Take the ratty houses, sell them for a little profit and keep the good houses. The increased discount will be worth the trouble and expense of disposing of the bad ones.

> **DEXTIP**
>
> Ask the asset manager, "How much of a better price will you give me if I buy three instead of one? And I will take that condo that has been sitting on your list for eight months."

Expedited Financing

Not all banks offer expedited financing, but it is well worth it if they do. To move the inventory off their list, banks will offer easy financing with pretty good terms. If the banks don't have many REOs, they are less inclined to offer financing because they do not have to. It is worth asking for.

The low down payment loans of only 5% are mostly a thing of the past, but one lender I know will offer it to investors for all of their REOs. For awhile, before the ALT-A loan revolution hit, this was the only way I could get a loan. Qualifying for this loan was extremely simple. One REO lender offered me a low rate, called me an "experienced investor," gave me 5 % down and closed the loan in five days!

Some banks would never think of loaning on a foreclosed property again, but others almost prefer it.

The Bank Realtor

Realtors who list a lot of bank properties are a special breed. Banks are looking for someone who can handle their sometimes arcane way of doing things. When the market is hot and times are good, bank brokers have to do other things to generate business. But when the market slows, they can be the main game in town.

Almost all banks use Realtors exclusively these days so you will make your initial offer through them. Most of them are wary of investors who waste their time with low-ball offers, but don't let that turn you off from making low offers on the right property.

REO Realtors can be quite an asset for you because they want to get paid, and they should have a pretty good idea how low the bank will go. Don't be afraid to ask them the lowest offer the bank will take—then offer less. By this time you should have done your due diligence and have run comparables (more about how to do that later).

You must also know your plans for the property:

1. What is your job description for the property?
2. If it is your plan to resell, how long (within days) will it take? (Explore my later chapter on flipping property.)
3. Do you know within a few hundred dollars what it will take to fix up?
4. If you plan to rent it out, exactly how much rent will you get?
5. How quickly will you get the house rented?
6. Do you know how to select a quality tenant who will:
   a. pay the rent on time?
   b. be a good steward of the asset?
   c. get along with the neighbors?
   d. stay a long time?

For an REO agent, dealing with investors is a cakewalk compared to the struggles they can have messing around with the banks' busy and chaotic asset management departments.

Many times when the Realtor gets the listing, it is a matter of hurry up and wait. It can be weeks before the bank will:

> **DEXTIP**
> Exploit the bank's inefficiencies by being firm and determined. Stay with it. Make the first offer when a property hits the market.

1. Pay them for a BPO
2. Get a lockbox on the house
3. Pay the Realtor to get the utilities turned on
4. Get an appraiser out there
5. Agree on what needs to be fixed up
6. Come up with a price

ابر an offer (if there is an investor that owns the loan, approving the initial offer will take much longer)
8. After escrow is opened, approve any buyer contingencies

I'm sure most bank brokers will agree that asset managers can be bureaucratic boneheads. Since they are so inefficient, a persistent investor who is out there writing a bunch of offers will win the day.

One of the most important pieces of advice I can give you is to cultivate, nourish and maintain your relationship with the bank Realtor, as well as with the asset manager at the bank.

Six Ways to Tell How Badly the Bank Wants to Sell

When you make an offer to the bank, you should definitely have these following factors in mind. How much of a discount you get from the bank depends on:

1. Time of the year you buy
2. Timing of the market cycle
3. Condition of the property
4. How long it has been on the market
5. How many other properties are for sale in the neighborhood
6. How thick the bank's inventory list is

Time of Year

Some REO gurus say that banks have better deals at the end of their fiscal year. The thinking is that they want to make their shareholders' report look better by disposing of non-performing assets and get them off of their balance sheets.

I asked one bank asset manager, who sold me a property that closed the day after Christmas, why they let me have it for eighty cents on the dollar. Was it because it was the end of their fiscal year? She just shrugged her shoulders and said, "Nobody else wanted it." But I got a Christmas present valued at $70,000 below market.

I'm not so sure how accurate that end-of-fiscal-year argument is, given that they will soon be awash in a mountain of REO property, if they are not already. The urgency the bank feels will not be from the shareholders—it will be from the Fed and Wall Street investors.

> **DEXTIP**
> Keep your powder dry and be ready to buy. Unpredictable Wall Street investors will start dumping property soon!

Nobody but the bank's board of directors will know exactly when the governmental regulators will come in and say, "You've got to sell it all now or we are cutting you off. Any new money you borrow will cost you more." For every bank, it will depend on its overall financial health. But that time will come, so be ready.

Private investors, be they Wall Street hedge funds, overseas investors or foreign central banks, will make their own call. It will be very interesting to see how soon they will pull the plug to get their money back. This is the joker in the deck because we have never seen so many foreigners and wealthy individuals holding so much of both our mortgage debt and governmental debt.

Timing of the Market Cycle

Everybody wants to buy at the precise bottom of the market cycle, when property values are at their lowest. The trouble is, nobody knows when that exact moment happens. You can recognize market bottoms only when you have passed them and savvy market timers get fooled all the time.

> **DEXTIP**
> Would you pick up a $100,000 bill if you saw it lying there in the street?

Banks know that we have come through a crazy, hysterical and euphoric real estate market in most areas of the country, fueled by Frankenstein loans and easy money. Banks have contributed to a national price hangover, and we must help them work off their bloated excess. Now, most areas are stagnant at best, and prices will decline. You may need to remind them about how bad the market is and tell them about:

1. Weakening sales volume
2. No first-time homebuyers entering the market
3. How prices will go down further
4. No recovery in sight
5. Boarded up houses showing up in neighborhoods
6. Listings exploding
7. More out-of-state migration
8. How most people have given up on real estate

If you are going to quickly buy and sell, your time horizon should be six months out at best. Make sure you buy low enough to give yourself a safety buffer. If you are buying property to hold for the long term, timing is less important. In the long-term scheme of things, is that extra $50,000 discount off the price less important than the fact that you DO buy REO houses and get started?

What is vital in negotiating price with the banks is how far below market value you can get it. Would you buy a house $100,000 below market value? Seventy-five thousand dollars below? Fifty thousand? If it was in a prime neighborhood and was going to make for a good rental, I might even pay close to retail. If I was going to rehab it and sell it for retail, location is not so important but price is. If I got a REALLY good deal, I would buy the house, provided it is not in a war zone.

Ten Signs the Market Bottom Has Passed
Maybe you want to start buying if you think the price cycle has hit bottom and prices are starting to ascend (just make sure it is not a false bottom). Here is what to look for when prices start their upward trend (and they will):

1. Monthly sales volume is increasing
2. More first-time homebuyers entering the market
3. Still a lot of naysayers saying prices will go down further
4. Recovery is "patchy"—not all areas are recovering at the same time
5. Monthly foreclosure rate declining
6. Sideways price trend—"choppy" and hard-to-discern direction
7. Listings decrease
8. More in-migration from out-of-state
9. Surrounding states' home prices are higher
10. Most people have given up on real estate

Condition of Property
We have already hit upon this, but the uglier, the better. When talking to the bank, I'll get a property inspector to go through the house with a fine tooth comb. Use that printed report as a negotiating tool then get the repairs done more cheaply.

How Long on the Market
The longer a property has been sitting on its REO list, the more money the bank is losing. Pressure to reduce price intensifies as the property's market age increases. When properties sit longer, they:

1. Become magnets for vandals and squatters
2. Deteriorate when nobody is living in them

3.   Have to compete with other bank listings
4.   Cause neighborhoods to decline in quality

Knowing this, make your offer accordingly. You can find out how long it has
been on the market from the Realtor, or pull a property profile from your local
title company. You can see the actual date when the title to the house changed
to the bank's name. That, along with how long it took to get the borrower out
of the house, is how long the bank has been losing money.

Sometimes the bank will practically beg you to take a property off their
hands. One REO manager I know asked if I remembered a certain house. I
said I did and she said, "I seriously want you to make an offer on that house. I
REALLY want you to."

I did not make an offer because it was not a keeper neighborhood. I did
not want to hold a property there for a long time because it was in a 'C' quality
area. I was picky about the neighborhood and you should be, too, if it is going
to be a long-term buy-and-hold. If it is a quick flip or a slow flip, neighborhood
quality is not so important.

Lots of Other Listings in the Neighborhood
A sea of "For Sale" signs definitely will keep that REO house on the market
longer. There is a good chance the bank won't know this and you should bring
it to their attention. When you make your below-market offer, I would include
a list of all of the other houses for sale so the bank knows that its only way to
make a sale is to chop its price.

"Average market time" is a stat that tells us, at the given pace of selling
houses, how long it will take to sell the entire given inventory. The longer the
time, the more money the bank will lose. If the average market time is over six
months, traditional wisdom holds that the market is a buyers' market.

When many houses are for sale, most asset managers know that REOS
have to be the lowest-priced house in the neighborhood. Bank foreclosures
lead the downward price spiral in every neighborhood. You need to make sure
that is the case because the asset managers know the only way to sell them is
to reduce the price.

How Thick the Bank's Inventory List Is
Call it a perverse pleasure, but when I see more REOs being added to the bank's
list of inventory, it makes me salivate like a chained-up dog. I can't wait to
chomp down on all the good deals—and that list expands daily.

Asset managers, who are trying to dispose of their laggard inventory in the most chaotic department at the bank, know it, too. They are hiring more employees, training inexperienced staff, losing track of houses and dealing with real estate agents they don't know. Each asset manager has a certain number of houses they are in charge of; as that work burden increases, houses can fall through the cracks and tempers get frayed.

> **DEXTIP**
> Scour the bank's inventory list every day to find below-market deals.

Every bank has a website where you can track its inventory flow. Work those websites every day; keep making offers and expose the inefficiencies. Ultimately, the bank will make a mistake to your advantage.

Conclusion

The more you know about a bank's motivation to sell a property, the better deal you will make. The bank wants to dispose of its unsold inventory that has been languishing on the market for months and that has to compete with a lot of other lower- priced listings, especially if it is the wrong buying season.

Keep in mind that the bank is seeing its fix-up money flying out the door, maintaining a deteriorating asset to keep it in saleable condition, paying insurance on a vacant house, paying the light bill, losing the opportunity to lend out that money and getting local advice from untested real estate agents who may not know what they are doing. All of this will work to your advantage when negotiating.

CHAPTER 10

REOs You Should and Shouldn't Buy—Be Wise With Your Time and Treasure

Just because an REO property is offered for sale at a low price doesn't mean you should buy it. That property may have undergone foreclosure for a good reason, and if there is an undiscovered defect or an undisclosed property flaw, it could cost you. I remember one foreclosure I didn't buy that was close to the whistlestop of nearby railroad tracks. Everything else was perfect about the house: it was in a great neighborhood, of newer construction and near a golf course. Had I not been there that evening while I was negotiating with the seller, I might have missed it.

Train whistles blasting in your ear at midnight is what you call a locally repugnant factor. You do not want to waste time on properties that do not fit your goals, or buy into bad neighborhoods. Nor do you want to deal with a bank that is not willing to listen to you. So in this chapter and the next, we will explore some deal-breakers:

> **DEXTIP**
> If you are going to buy and hold a portfolio of quality properties that will stay fully rented, know that your tenants will look like your houses.

1. Bad locations
2. Wrong property
3. Alligators (and I don't mean in the backyard)
4. Bank is not willing to deal

Bad Locations

The first properties that appear in the initial wave of bank foreclosures always seem to be the ratty ones that nobody wants:

1. In the boondocks or too far away from the job centers where renters work. These properties may be in foreclosure for good reason because they are not in the best locations.
2. Lower-priced multi-unit properties in transitional neighborhoods. Tough to manage, lots of ongoing fix-up.
3. Properties that are commercially adjacent. It's tough to market properties that are next door to commercial enterprises.

Those who rent your house want the same things you do: safety, security, close access to freeways to get to their nearby jobs, and a sense of community. Buying REOs nowadays can be a minefield. Many of them are located in areas of high subprime loan concentration, where first-time homebuyers can buy cheap. And sometimes cheap ain't good.

Older neighborhoods can be magnets for crime, delinquency and drug problems. It is extremely important to identify neighborhood trends. Watch out if you see:

- Yards not being kept up
- Businesses going under
- Vacant storefronts
- Houses in a state of disrepair
- Cars parked in yards
- Deteriorating fences
- Pawnshops
- Paycheck cashing places
- Grocery store carts
- Congested street parking with lots of grease spots
- A large number of rental houses

But neighborhoods change. Every neighborhood has a life cycle called gentrification. It is how the neighborhood ages itself. The neighborhood can stay the same, deteriorate and go downhill, or improve in value. This improvement is called resurgence. Signs that a neighborhood is resurging include:

- Neighborhood is starting to look better
- New people are moving in
- Older homes are being fixed up or torn down
- Rise in owner occupants
- Younger families are walking the sidewalks with dogs and baby strollers
- Banks and franchises are moving in
- New businesses are being started
- Home Depot, Starbucks, nice restaurants are opening

However, I also don't like out-of-state neighborhoods that I cannot drive to. I say if you cannot afford to walk around your neighborhood (and keep an eye on things), you can't afford it. The main trouble is that out-of-area property management does not watch my money like I do, and I have to rely on too many people I do not know. I may like a certain city's economic future, and it may seem ripe for growth, but who knows if I'll benefit?

My out-of-sight investment may be on the wrong side of town, or have a manager who steals from me. Besides, with local properties becoming cheaper by the minute, who needs to go out of town?

Neighborhoods I Like (Andy Griffith's Mayberry, R.F.D.)

After all that being said, I love older neighborhoods. They're safe, mature and have character. I prefer them because they are cheaper. Those pride-of-ownership neighborhoods' cash flows are better, they are usually close to where there are lots of jobs and people are moving in, and REOs thereappreciate as well as any other house in the area. The best part is that loads of REOs show up in these places.

Tree-lined streets are great, although trees in your

DEXTIP

Buying well located houses in high-demand neighborhoods eliminates the biggest real estate risk because in good times and bad, there will always be somebody who will want to rent or buy your house. Pride-of-ownership neighborhoods have withstood the test of time.

yard shed leaves, windstorms break off their limbs, and they die. Go for low-maintenance shrubbery or small trees.

I think neighborhoods are like banks: they are so important as storehouses of value and money. People don't buy houses, they buy *neighborhoods* and renters are the same way. Why wouldn't you want to have the best bank possible?

Houses I Don't Like (Pot Farms, Gambling Houses, Barnyards and Condos)

With bank foreclosures, you get all types. I've seen chicken coops and backyard barnyards, rabbit farms and in-house gambling places set up like casinos. I walked through bank foreclosures that were customized beyond marketability, and hydrophonic pot farms with the high-intensity light fixtures still hanging and the strong smell of weed still there. These abodes are what you call non-congruent houses for the neighborhood.

If you are going to flip these personalized structures, then you will have to bring them up to neighborhood standards to sell them. That's a lot of trouble. If you are going to hold them, break out your wallet.

If the house is all the way fixed up, you can be sure the bank will expect a retail price to get its money out of the structure. It is better to find one in which they have made just a few cosmetic repairs and it still needs a lot of work. If the property is in move-in condition, you are probably wasting your time.

In the early stages of the price cycle, banks are thinking retail price, but don't let that stop you from making a low offer. As they start loading up on non-performing assets, they will see that there is little return on their fix-up money. And you will see more dog-eared property that you can make deals on. Although how much they like to fix them up differs from bank to bank, the more mature the REO market, the rattier the houses get.

I do not like condominiums for investment purposes. Here is why:

1. HOA (home owner association) assessments are always going up and there is little you can do about it.
2. HOAs do not like absentee owners who usually vote against special assessments and increased dues to maintain and improve the condo complex.
3. Restrictions on use of the common areas
4. Not tenant friendly
5. Not kid friendly

6. They do not like dogs—and if you limit dogs, you greatly limit the potential rental market. I never had a dog stiff me for rent.
7. Tenants move in and out of condos more often.
8. Lack of storage and parking
9. Smaller square footage
10. If you are trying to sell in soft markets, you will have lots of company.
11. Rents held down by competitive rentals in the same building
12. Older condos have trouble competing with newer condo projects in the area.
13. Condo projects that are full of renters get beat up more.
14. Lenders do not like renter-saturated condo projects. It's hard to get loans if the building is over 40%-50% renter-occupied.

Condos' Main Advantages Are:

1. Affordability—Since they are cheap, they may be all you can afford. REOs show up much more frequently since they lose value more rapidly in soft markets because of the above shortcomings.
2. Lack of exterior upkeep—This lifestyle advantage of not having to worry about the outside maintenance is ideal for retirees who want to "lock and leave," and cash-strapped young people also like this benefit.
3. Great for your first home—If all you can afford is a condo for your first home, it is worth it because it gets you into the game.

> **DEXTIP**
> Since REO single-family homes can go well below market value, condos can get really cheap.

In addition, there are other properties I don't like. Commercially-adjacent areas are never good places to have long-term rentals. The noise, congestion and pollution mean renters do not stay long, and you have to watch your zoning for illegal added-on units, sleeping room additions or garage conversions. REOs seem to show up more here but they do not make great rentals. You may have future trouble from the city and lenders may not lend on them. An unpermitted addition may present a future fire and safety hazards.

Flippers may want an REO in the middle of a major renovation. It is very common to see owners overspend on a house remodel and run out of money; then it goes back to the bank. Some minor repairs are okay but you do not want to see bare drywall, cement floors or electrical wires hanging unless you get a great price and you are handy.

Odd room configurations are hard to overcome. Odd layouts that do not conform to other properties in the area will not be marketable. Houses with unusual floor plans can make the house more prone to a bank foreclosure because they are tough to sell.

If the home's square footage is too large or too small for the neighborhood and it is not compatible with surrounding housing, it affects future marketability and can be foreclosure material.

Don't buy rural property. Houses on large acreages with not many other houses around it are hard to sell and tough to rent.

Keep away from homes with pools (if the tenant's little kid drowns, they're coming after you). There is also extra maintenance expense.

Finally, I don't like houses with flat roofs. Rainwater collects there and they leak more often.

Houses I Do Like

These include no expensive ones and no really cheap ones. In most REO markets, no price segment is safe. Bank foreclosures show up on every block.

High-dollar places where the well heeled can swing wildly may seem like REO bargains, and if you have the stomach for a high-end flip, there could be a big payday (pay particular attention to the upcoming section on flipping REOs). Although there is a very good chance that multi-million-dollar mansions will show up on REO lists, big negative cash flows and helpless yuppie tenants can make buying these palaces an expensive management nightmare. They are also harder to rent. If you've got the bucks, however, they can appreciate extremely well. You can often get them for many hundreds of thousands below market and can flip these if you know what you are doing.

I like well-located, three-bedroom, two-bathroom houses averaging 1,100-1,600 square feet, situated in pride-of-ownership neighborhoods. I like upper-blue collar tenants who can do things with their hands.

> **DEXTIP**
> Flippers take note: Buying single- family houses at wholesale prices and being able to quickly retail them at full price to an owner-occupant buyer makes this booming REO market a monumental opportunity.

Two-bedroom houses are too small; tenants get crowded and don't stay long, and the house gets a lot of wear. Houses with more than three bedrooms attract big, blended families and it costs the tenant more to heat and cool them. Big families wear out houses. No one-bathroom houses, either, because that bathroom will get too much use. In short, I buy houses my tenants love to live in.

Older houses have wall panel heating and window air conditioners. That suits me just fine because they are inexpensive to maintain, break down less, and are cheaper for the tenant to operate.

At What Price?

Take the median house price for your town and buy up to 25% below it. The rent/price ratio is better and this price appeals to the largest segment of the renting and buying public, plus houses in this price range appreciate as well as any other house in your town.

I've always done well in this middle to lower-middle range of the market, and if you are first starting out, focus on the cheapest property you can get in the best neighborhood.

However, I must confess that with this raging REO market, I am going to go for nicer houses because of the bargains that will be there. Making this move to nicer, higher-end type of houses is wise; always try to upgrade the quality of your buy and hold portfolio. Top-of-the-line houses:

1. Are better built and better designed
2. Can get a better bargain if you buy them "on sale"
3. Need less maintenance
4. Are in –'A' neighborhoods
5. Can attract helpless tenants

Alligators

Rents that don't come close to your payment (too much negative cash flow) are alligators that can eat you alive. I'm willing to take a modest negative if I know area rents are expected to appreciate. That's why I buy the low- to middle-range houses close to or on the edge of major job centers because the rents go up there and so do the house values.

Knowing which properties to buy is important; knowing how to get the cash flow and loans with which to buy them is essential. Let's take a look in the next chapter.

CHAPTER 11

Negative Cash Flow's Dirty Little Secret

The number one reason people don't invest in houses (besides lack of knowledge) is lack of money for a down payment and the inability to withstand negative cash flow. You really need to find a way to deal with this or you will never buy.

Everybody says, "Yeah, but you can't do that in California. Too much negative cash flow." I said that myself until I read a gem of a book written by my mentor, Dr. David Schumacher, called, *Buy and Hold: 7 Steps to a Real Estate Fortune*. I quote: " It takes knowledge to accumulate real estate and the guts to put yourself on the line. You have to be disciplined and careful not to overextend yourself." Dr. Schumacher continues, "Many times I didn't have the money to pay the taxes. I scraped the bottom more than once."

I couldn't have said it better. Sacrificing and delaying gratification are values that need to be rediscovered so you can take care of your real estate until it can take care of you.

It has always been tough to get positive cash flow from investment real estate located in expensive states. When you buy a big asset

> **DEXTIP**
> Astute investors know that there are many ways to combat negative cash flow, especially if you buy in areas of high job growth where rents rise.

like real estate with maximum leverage and low down payments, most houses will not have a positive cash flow at first. That's just the way it is.

If you buy in the pricier coastal communities, crowded urban areas or more expensive resort destinations where real estate appreciates well, rents never grow as much as local housing values. Rents never keep up, at least not at the same time. When housing prices spiral out of sight, fewer people can buy so they rent. When housing gets to be too expensive and the prices begin their inevitable decline, guess what? Rents go up, and keep going up until buying a house becomes affordable again.

The most common ways in which investors deal with negative cash flow are all variations of:

1. Tough it out until property rents rise past the monthly nut.
2. Investor has a big down payment.
3. Seller agrees to put some of the equity on the sidelines (i.e., seller carries a second mortgage with no payments).
4. Exotic and possibly risky financing
5. Buy lower-priced property in possibly less commercially dynamic areas (out of state or remote areas). Watch out—they may take longer to rent and may not appreciate well.
6. Add income value to the investment (add more income units, rent out rooms and garages).
7. Buy commercial property or apartment units.
8. Buy good property at big discounts in areas of economic vibrancy.

If you are just starting out, or you don't have money, you will need to be creative. Buying under-market REO property may be your best chance at getting into the game.

I wrote an article for a national real estate magazine outlining negative cash flow busters. Here are twenty-five ways to deal with negative cash flow:

1. Shop your insurance premiums. Go for the lowest-priced quote you can find from a reputable company.
2. Raise your insurance deductibles to $1,000, $2,000 or more. You may get an argumentative letter from your lender but it is well worth a try.
3. Fine tune your coverages. I heard of one investor who trimmed volcanic damage from his policy and saved a bundle. Most people never read their insurance policies.

4. Don't over-insure. You only need insurance for the actual housing structure, not the land. I know this sounds elementary, but you would be surprised.
5. Have your property re-assessed. If your area is declining in value, call the county tax assessor, as many Californians did in the 1990s, to save a bundle.

Increase Your Personal Income

6. Strongly focus on your job or business to massively increase your personal income and feed your negative cash flow properties. Real estate markets are always in flux, so those who survive to hang on to their quality "keeper" properties will prosper.
7. Raise your rents to the market. Rents are going up around the country as housing becomes more expensive so call around to several different property managers to find the going rate in your area.

Take on a Cash Partner

8. Increase income by selling a piece of the upside to a cash investor. He can give you a one-time cash lump sum or give you cash in monthly installments to offset your monthly negative cash flow.
9. A cash investor could be attracted to your deal because you bought it at discount. You also have intact equity to barter with because you bought it at discount. Look for cash-rich Roth IRAs or regular self-directed IRAs to offer the investor an attractive yield he cannot get elsewhere, or sell a partial percentage.

Add Income Value to Your Investment

10. Rent out your garage for storage.
11. Convert your garage to an extra bedroom.
12. Rent out your property by the room (college students come to mind).
13. Change the use of your property to special needs housing or to a board and care facility. The old, disabled, mentally challenged and drug/alcohol dependent are just some of those suffering severe housing shortages. Social workers know governmental programs that will pay housing expenses for the medically afflicted.

14. Build in additional square footage (a bedroom, for example) that will gain a higher rent.

15. Renegotiate management fees by a giving your property manager a piece of the action. Modify your management relationship to a partnership by exchanging monthly fees for equity.

16. Up your tax benefits by becoming a full-time real estate investor to escape the limited $25,000 federal capital loss exclusion. Go to *www.irs.gov* to look up requirements, but be careful because the word on the street is that they are cracking down. (*http://www.irs.gov/businesses/small/article/0,,id=146825,00.html*)

If You Have to Sell but Are Having Trouble

17. Keep and rent out the good houses and dump the bad ones.

18. Lease option: Advertise your property as "rent to own." Sell your property via lease option and get upfront money plus much higher rent, part of which is credited to the buyer's down payment should he exercise his option.

19. Do a 1031 tax deferred exchange into an income property, like an apartment building, or into higher-rent areas where the price to rent ratios are better.

20. Offer a higher commission (4%-5%) as an incentive to the buyer's agent. Your house gets shown first.

21. Use creative financing to sell your property on terms for a long-term stream of income. You will become a lender instead of an owner by using wrap around mortgages, installment sales and AITDs that convert equity into income. Owners carrying mortgages to sell property in soft markets were once commonplace and will be again.

22. You are a lender when you creatively finance. As a lender, you can offer a low price and a zero down payment in exchange for marked up interest rates.

In the Future

23. Buy low. Unless you can buy from a builder in distress, stay away from overpriced, brand new houses. Only buy resales in principally owner-occupied, pride-of-ownership neighborhoods that

are priced well below your town's median price. *This REO market affords you this opportunity.*

24. Deals will abound in areas of foreclosures and high seller distress so you will be able to buy well-located houses in high-demand neighborhoods (close to the work centers, shopping, and freeways that your customer, the renter, prefers). Position yourself to be credit rich and cash heavy.

25. Buy no investment condos, condo conversions or houses far outside of town. As markets turn soft, these properties sink first. A three-bedroom, two-bathroom single-family detached house is the most in-demand piece of real estate in this country today.

The Bank is Not Willing to Deal

When the REO surge first hits asset managers, especially if they are being fed inaccurate market information or if they are located out of state, they can be the most resistant and stubborn sellers you will meet. Here again, the bank's inefficiencies can be exploited.

> **DEXTIP**
> Wait out the banks. If they refuse your first offer, follow up several months later if it is a great house.

I would not waste time on a property where the bank has already rejected offers higher than what you were willing to pay. If they reject your offer, move on to the next house, but keep your eye on the initial one.

If after a few months the property is still for sale, re-enter negotiations. You may encounter a new set of ears that will listen to your offer. Turnover at the bank's frenzied asset management department, amplified pressure from regulators and dismal stock performance will make your persistent offers more welcomed.

How Do I Know How Much to Offer the Bank?

Rather than talking in abstractions about how much below market you should offer the bank, I want you to see how I would look at an actual bank property for sale. It is on the market as I am writing this, and here is the actual property profile that I pulled from the title company, as well as what nearby houses have sold for. The purchase price offered by the listing REO broker is $460,000. Is this a good deal? To determine that, I have put the most pertinent information in bold.

RESIDENTIAL FUNDING CO LLC; RESIDENTIAL FUNDING CORP,
Secondary Owner:
Mail Address:
Site Address: **2440 W GREENLEAF AVE**
                  ANAHEIM CA 92801
Assessor Parcel Number: 071-083-06
Census Tract: 0868.02
Housing Tract Number: 2390
Page Grid: 768 -C4
Legal Description: Tract No: 2390
Abbreviated Description: N TR 2390 LOT 87
Property Characteristics:
Bedrooms: 3   Year Built: 1955 Square Feet: 1,284 SF
Bathrooms: 1.5 Garage: Attached   Lot Size: 6,630 SF / 0.152 AC
Total Rooms: 7   Fireplace: Number of Units: 0
Zoning: Pool: Use Code: Single Family Residential
No. of Stories: 1 Latitude: 33.84221   Longitude: -117.9694
Building Style:
Sale & Loan Information:
Last Transfer Date: 11/17/2006   Seller: BARAJAS, RAUL
Transfer Value: $502,392

Let's recap the data that is most vital, then I will tell you why this REO might interest me. Here we have a three-bedroom, 1.5-bathroom house in Anaheim, CA, offered for sale by Residential Funding Corp. This 1,284-square-foot house was taken back by the bank on November 17, 2006, from the unfortunate Raul Barajas. The transfer amount was $502,392, which was probably the defaulted foreclosure amount or his loan balances. This is all we need to know.

The first thing that interests me is the date when the bank took the property back, November 17, 2006. The bank has had that property for eight and a half months, as of this writing. Wow, eight and a half months since the foreclosure sale date, and the lender has just now put this property on the market. The former owner, Raul Barajas, probably became a tenant and the bank had to evict him. Then they had to clean it up, repair it, pay the old utility bill, get a BPO, probably do an appraisal, pay the broker to list it, and keep the collateral in good repair.

The bank took it in the shorts on this one. This lender has had no payments since November 17, 2006, and probably four to six months before that. Plus, the bank is taking another hit because the listing price is $460,000, over $40,000 less than what was owed.

If you look at the comparable sales data (comps), you will see that the bank really wants to get rid of this house, which is priced about $75,000 under what other similar property is selling for in the neighborhood. Let's look at the recent sales data:

Comparable Sales Data

No.	Address	Date	Price	$/SF	Bld/Area	RM/BR/Bth	YB	Lot Area	Pool	Proxim.
	Subject Property	11/17/2006	$502,392	$391	**1,284**	/3/1.5	1955	6,630 SF		
1	1005 N MODENA PL	06/26/2007	$535,000	$419	1276	7/4/2.0	1955	6,000 SF		.23Mi.
2	719 N ROANNE ST	12/22/2006	$590,000	$456	1293	7/3/2.0	1955	6,209 SF		.14Mi.
3	701 N GILBERT ST	11/01/2006	$552,000	$422	1309	7/4/2.0	1955	6,200 SF		.10Mi.
4	804 N GENEVA ST	10/02/2006	$680,000	$595	1143	6/3/1.5	1955	6,200 SF		.15Mi.
5	827 N ROANNE ST	09/29/2006	$575,000	$451	1275	7/4/2.0	1959	6,480 SF		.06Mi.
6	718 N GENEVA ST	08/29/2006	$565,000	$440	1284	7/3/1.5	1955	6,200 SF		.15Mi.

Comp #1, which sold one month previously for $535,000, is the best comp; it is of recent vintage (June 26, 2007), is nearby (.23 miles away) and is of similar square footage (1,276). So is the true value around $535,000?

Perhaps, perhaps not. Notice how old the other comps are, from August 29, 2006, to December 22, 2006. Nothing else has sold within a half-mile for *six months.* And when they were selling, the values were $552,000 to $680,000.

> **DEXTIP**
> Are sales comparables trending up or down in your town?

So what does that tell us? It shows that the price trend is heading down, and the bank knows it. RFC Bank has a clue, and Realtors who have listings from many other banks also confirm that this is the case.

Local Price Trends

Would I buy it? Price-wise, I think values in these areas have further to fall. This property did ultimately sell for $460,000 (a great wholesale price) but it looks like the sales comps are getting lower. Prices trending lower are something you always have to watch out for. For somebody who is looking to live there for a long time, it's hard to go wrong by buying a home below market value. As a pure investment, though, I would wait.

Why wait? It's a slow market when:

1. There's a big backlog of houses (months of inventory are growing)
2. Nobody's buying (sales volume are down)
3. Lots of people are not making their house payments (the sheer number of NODs being filed is up)
4. More people than usual are in trouble (the rate of people going into default is up)
5. People can't pay the taxes, either (the county tax assessor says that property tax payments are increasingly delinquent)
6. "For sale" signs are staying up (days on the market and listing times keep going up)
7. Sellers have got to cut prices to stand a chance (price reductions are everywhere)
8. REOs show up on your block
9. Many people are leaving the state (net out-migration)

These market indicators reveal the health in any real estate market. When I see any one of these indicators change, my ears prick up…then I might buy that property above.

Banks Are Starting to be More Flexible on Price

Banks listen to their REO brokers, who give them the above market parameters so they know where to set prices. Banks are starting to price their propertiesbelow their initial BPO, and REO agents are telling me that their opinion of prices is always on the low side. Realtors who scale their value opinions on the low side don't want to be stuck with a slew of overpriced bank listings that are not selling and are falling more behind the price trend.

A good question to ask the REO broker is which of his client banks is being the most aggressive.

> **DEXTIP**
> Ask the REO broker which lenders act like they really want to sell. Then just focus on those lenders.

CHAPTER 12

Making Your Offer

Okay, we have talked about why there are so many REOs, where to find them and who will talk with you about them. You now want to know how to end up with the houses on your terms, and what an actual bank purchase transaction looks like.

Making an offer to the bank is not like dealing with ordinary private sellers. You can expect the bank to:

1. Have no face-to-face negotiation
2. Take a long time to accept your offer
3. Not work weekends or nights
4. Operate with no rhyme or reason
5. Be skeptical of you

For me, working with the banks was actually a pleasure. Mostly, they were very professional and we talked the same lingo. Nobody got testy or nasty. But I had no compunction about offering a LOW price the first time around. They countered with a higher offer. I put my final offer in this letter of intent:

LETTER OF INTENT

July 13, 2001
American Savings
Attention: Summer or Anne
RE: OFFER TO PURCHASE 11622 ACACIA STREET, GARDEN GROVE, CA

I would like to purchase the house at 11622 Acacia Street in Garden Grove, CA.

I am a well-qualified real estate agent who has many years of experience purchasing single-family homes. I hold them and fix them up for long-term use.

I look forward to owning and bringing Acacia Street up to excellent condition to reflect the pride of ownership I saw in the neighborhood.

However, I have found that much-needed repairs are necessary to bring it up to that standard. They are:

Needs interior and exterior paint
Roof may need replacing, due to water damage throughout the house
Carpets need to be replaced Kitchen cabinets and counters need replacing
Water heater is disconnected
House has dry rot and termite damage
Possible mold damage
Window screens need replacing
House needs to be cleaned up
Lawn is dead and needs landscaping
Needs new window treatments (blinds)
Active live bee infestation in backyard presents safety hazard

I will buy the house for $200,500.00 and would like to take advantage of your loan program at 7.125% interest, fixed for 30 years. I have a high FICO score and am well-qualified. I could close escrow in 30 days or less or whatever is convenient for you.

Please fax back your answer to me at XXX-XXX-XXXX or call me at XXX-XXX-XXXX. It is okay to talk to Susan if I am not in when you call.
Thank you.

My first verbal offer was $175,000. The market price for this house, if it was fixed up, was about $249,000. I listed all the things wrong with the house, supplied estimated costs to fix it up (estimating on the high side), and had the property inspected top to bottom. We gave them a copy of the inspection report. Your offer should include an inspection contingency period that allows you to terminate the sale if the inspections reveal unanticipated damages that the bank will not correct.

The bank did not want to lose the deal when we found some more dry rot. We saved an additional $3,500 since they did not want to put the property back on the market.

By the end of the process, we definitely knew the house better than they did. It cost us $15,000 to bring it to rent-able shape, and we did not do all the repairs. Since we were into the house for $212,000, you might think that getting this house for only 15% below market value is not a deal. Our payment (PITI) was $1,577. It only rented for $1,350 a month, making for a $227 negative cash flow.

WOW. You mean to tell me that a $227 negative cash flow REO property bought only 15% below market value is a deal? Why is this such a good deal? Let me count the ways:

1.   We got $36,000 intact equity.
2.   The area was appreciating 10% a year in 2001.
3.   Rents in that neighborhood are now $2,100 a month.
4.   Loan principal is now paid over $13,000.
5.   It was a great pride-of-ownership neighborhood.
6.   We pay $2,100 less income tax.
7.   It was close so we could manage it ourselves.
8.   It will always rent easily.
9.   Property is now worth $625,000.

Banks Now Use Teams

The bank/asset manager has potentially thousands of properties, and the only way to dispose of them in an efficient manner is to follow set procedures.

Most banks/firms use "teams" or department sections to complete the

> **DEXTIP**
> Banks are simply not prepared to break their routines, or re-route personnel for a single property. It wouldn't be worth the increased liability or man-hours. You are just part of the overall process. Be patient, and take advantage.

following tasks as quickly and efficiently as possible. THIS IS ONLY A PARTIAL DESCRIPTION:

With these thousands of properties, they must concern themselves with occupant issues, safety and hazard issues, legal and title issues, property preservation issues, expense management, documentation and company/lender auditors, investor oversight, potential insurance claims, PMI or M/I claims, government oversight, Fair Housing issues and profit/loss (values). This doesn't even include the things to come when it's time to actually list, sell and close on the property: someone's got to review the HUDs, answer the phone calls and count the money.

I'd add one other thing. On most properties, with most banks and asset management firms, a listing agent is assigned within one to seven days after foreclosure. This is done to quickly determine and resolve any occupant issues, secure the property (no trespassing), halt code violation fines and, as importantly, to prevent further deterioration of the property and rectify any public safety issues (i.e., if someone gets hurt on the property minutes after the foreclosure sale, guess who's responsible?)

Offers are usually faxed to the bank. If you are using an agent to prepare your offer, he will probably want to use his own Board of Realtors form. If you are making your own offer directly to the bank, use the form below. It is a standard purchase offer form, and any bank should accept it.

> **DEXTIP**
> Find foreclosures ahead of the pack. Some companies even assign an agent prior to foreclosure sale because they know what they are getting back. Building relationships with agents like these is invaluable.

STANDARD REAL ESTATE PURCHASE AND SALE AGREEMENT
FOR AGREEMENT FOR DEED PROPERTY

Parties _____
(hereinafter referred to as "Buyer"), and

_____
(hereinafter referred to as "Seller"), which terms may be singular or plural and will include the heirs, successors, personal representatives and assigns of Seller and Buyer, hereby agree that Seller will sell and Buyer will buy the following property, with such improvements as are located thereon, and is described as follows: All that tract of land lying and being in Land Lot _____ of the_____ District, _____ Section of _____ County, _____ and being known as Address: _____ City: _____ State: _____ Zip: _____ according to the present system of numbering in and around this area, and being more particularly described as Lot _____, Block _____, Unit _____, Phase/Section _____ of _____ Subdivision, as recorded in Plat Book _____, Page _____, _____ County, _____ records together with all light fixtures, appliances, all electrical, mechanical, plumbing, air-conditioning, and any other systems or fixtures as are attached thereto; all plants, trees, and shrubbery now a part thereof, together with all the improvements thereon; and all appurtenances thereto, all being hereinafter collectively referred to as the "Property." The full legal description of said Property is the same as is recorded with the Clerk of the Superior Court of the County in which the Property is located and is made a part of this Agreement by reference.

Seller will sell and Buyer will buy upon the following terms and conditions, if completed or marked. On any conflict of terms or conditions, that which is added will supersede that which is printed or marked. It is understood that the Property will be conveyed by an Agreement for Deed, with covenants, restrictions, and easements of record.

1. **Total Purchase Price** to be paid by Buyer is payable as follows:
   A. Earnest money deposit, which will remain as a binder until closing, unless sooner forfeited or returned, according to the provisions of this Agreement.
      $_____
   B. "Subject to" existing loan balance encumbering the Property
      (Approx. Bal..)
      $_____
      Lender _____ Loan #_____
      Interest Rate _____% Fixed Rate [ ] Adjustable Rate [ ]
      P&I $_____ per month
   C. "Subject to" existing loan balance encumbering the Property
      (Approx. Bal..)
      $_____
      Lender _____ Loan #_____
      Interest Rate _____% Fixed Rate [ ] Adjustable Rate [ ]
      P&I $_____ per month
   D. Balance due at closing:
      approximately [   ] exactly [   ]
      $_____
   E. Total Purchase Price.
      approximately [   ] exactly [   ]
      $_____

2. **Seller Will Pay:** Seller will pay all closing costs to include; Recording Fees, Intangibles Tax, Credit Reports, Funding Fee, Loan Origination Fee, Document Preparation Fee, Loan Insurance Premium, Loan Discount, Title Insurance Policy, Attorney's Fees, Courier Fees, Overnight Fee, Appraisal Fee, Survey, Transfer Tax, Satisfaction and Recording Fees, Wood Destroying Organism Report and any other costs associated with the funding or closing of this Agreement; Buyer will pay all additional monies. All taxes, rentals, condominium or association fees, monthly mortgage insurance premiums and interest on loans will be prorated as of the date of closing.

3. **Payment of Expenses:** If Buyer fails to perform the completion of any required documentation, all loan and sale processing and closing costs incurred, whether the same were to be paid by Seller or Buyer, will be the responsibility of the Buyer, with costs deducted from binder deposit. If Seller fails to perform, all loan, sales processing and closing costs incurred, whether the same were to be paid by Seller or Buyer, will be the responsibility of Seller; and Buyer will be entitled to the return of the binder deposit. This will include, but shall not be limited to, the transaction not being closed because Seller is unwilling to complete the transaction, or because Seller elects not to pay for the excess amount in paragraph 9 (with respect to repairs), or because Seller cannot deliver marketable title.

4. **Escrow Accounts:** Seller herewith assigns Seller's escrow account (if any) and property hazard insurance policy, at no cost to Buyer.

5. **Wood Destroying Organism Report:** "Wood Destroying Organism" means any arthropod or plant life that damages a structure. Seller will have property inspected by a Certified Pest Control Firm to determine whether there is any visible active wood destroying organism infestation or visible existing structural damage from wood destroying organisms to the improvements. Buyer shall be provided with a copy of the report within seven (7) days of this Agreement and if either or both of the foregoing are present Seller will have seven (7) days from receipt of written notice thereof within which to have all such wood destroying organism damages, whether visible or not, inspected and estimated by a licensed building or general contractor. Seller shall pay all costs of treatment and repair of all structural damage up to three percent (3%) of the purchase price. If such costs exceed this amount, and Seller declines to treat and repair, Buyer will have the option of (a) terminating this Agreement and receiving a refund of any and all earnest money and credits paid or earned, or, (b) proceeding with the transaction, in which event Seller will bear costs equal to three percent (3%) of the purchase price.

6. **Title Examination and Time for Closing:** (**A**) If title evidence and survey show Seller is vested with a marketable title, subject to the usual exceptions contained in title insurance commitments (such as exceptions for survey, current taxes, zoning ordinances, covenants, restrictions and easements of record), the transaction will be closed and the Agreement for Deed and other closing papers delivered on or before _____, 20____ [ ], or _____ days after date of satisfaction of all conditions in paragraph 14 [ ], unless extended by other conditions of this Agreement or this agreement is canceled by the Buyer. (**B**) If title evidence or survey reveal any defects which render the title unacceptable to Buyer, Buyer will have seven (7) days from receipt of title commitment and survey to notify Seller of such title defects and Seller agrees to use reasonable diligence to cure such defects at Seller's expense and will have thirty (30) days to do so, in which event this transaction will be closed within ten (10) days after delivery to Buyer of evidence that such defects have been cured. During this period of delay, Buyer shall not be required to make any regular required payments if required under any other Agreement(s). If Seller is unable to convey to Buyer an acceptable title, Buyer will have the right to terminate this Agreement, and shall return to Seller all title evidence and surveys received from Seller; or Buyer will have the right to accept such title as Seller may be able to convey, and to close this transaction upon the terms stated herein, which election will be exercised within ten (10) days from notice of Seller's inability to cure. Seller agrees to pay for and discharge all due or delinquent taxes, liens and other encumbrances, unless otherwise agreed.

7. **Loss or Damage:** If the property is damaged by fire or other casualty prior to closing, and cost of restoration does not exceed three percent (3%) of the assessed valuation of the improvements located on the Property, cost of restoration will be an obligation of the Seller and closing will proceed when repairs are complete and acceptable to Buyer, pursuant to the terms of this Agreement with all costs therefore paid prior to closing. In the event cost of restoration exceeds three percent (3%) of the assessed valuation of the improvements and Seller declines to repair or restore, Buyer

will have the option of either taking the Property "as-is," together with either the said three percent (3%) or any insurance proceeds payable by virtue of such loss or damage, or of canceling this Agreement.

8. **Property Condition:** Seller agrees to deliver the Property in its **PRESENT "AS-IS" CONDITION** except as otherwise specified herein. Seller does hereby certify and represent that Seller has legal authority and capacity to convey the Property with all improvements. Seller further certifies and represents that Seller knows of no latent defects to the Property and knows of no facts materially affecting the value of the Property except as noted on the "Seller's Condition Report" made a part of this Agreement by reference. Buyer has inspected the Property and Buyer accepts the Property in its **PRESENT "AS-IS" CONDITION**, except as otherwise specified herein.

9. **Personal Property:** Included in the purchase price are all fixed equipment including ceiling fans, drapery hardware, attached lighting fixtures, mailbox, fence, plants, and shrubbery as now installed on the property, appliances including dishwasher, range, refrigerator, and these additional items:

_____
_____
_____. Items specifically excluded from this Agreement:
_____.

10. **Occupancy:** Seller represents that there are no parties in occupancy other than Seller, and Buyer will be given occupancy at closing unless occupancy is granted sooner pursuant to any other agreement(s) entered into by Buyer and Seller.

11. **Default and Attorney's Fees:** If Buyer defaults on this Agreement, all deposits will be retained by the Seller in settlement of any claim, as full liquidated damages, whereupon Buyer and Seller will be relieved of all obligations under this Agreement. If Seller defaults under this Agreement, the Buyer may seek specific performance or elect to receive the return of the Buyer's

binder deposit(s) without thereby waiving any action for damages resulting from Seller's breach. In connection with any litigation arising out of this Agreement, the prevailing party will be entitled to recover all costs including reasonable attorney's fees.

12. **Zoning and Restrictions:** The Property is zoned residential and Buyer will have ten (10) days from acceptance to verify the existing zoning and current proposed changes, and deliver written notice of objections to Seller or be deemed to have waived objections under this paragraph.

13. **Maintenance:** Until title is delivered, Seller agrees to maintain all heating, sewer, plumbing and electrical systems and any built in appliances and other equipment in normal working order and to keep the roof water tight and to maintain the grounds.

14. **SPECIAL STIPULATIONS**: The following stipulations shall control in the event of conflict with any of the foregoing.

15. **Agreements:** Buyer and Seller have entered into no other agreements, promises or understandings between these parties. This legal and binding Agreement will be construed under _____ Law and if not understood, parties should seek competent legal advice. **TIME IS OF ESSENCE IN THIS AGREEMENT.**

Signed, sealed and delivered on the _____ day of _____, 20_____.

_____(Seal)

_____(Seal)

Buyer: (Print or type Name) _____

Seller: (Print or type Name) _____

_____(Seal)

_____(Seal)

Buyer: (Print or type Name) _____

Seller: (Print or type Name) _____

Buying Your First Home

We have already covered buying bank foreclosed single-family houses for investment purposes, but what about buying your first home?

For you property virgins, this is your best chance to invest in your first residence. Houses (or condos, for first-timers) will not get more affordable than they will within the next few years. It is the smartest real estate investment you can make because:

1. You are not subject to the whims of a landlord who might:
   a. Raise the rent;
   b. Sell the house to an owner-occupant (so common within the last few years).
2. There is easy mortgage financing, in most cases.
3. A sound, well-located property has the highest potential appreciation.
4. There are tax deductions for interest and property taxes.
5. You get pride of ownership.

Perhaps you pay low rent where you live now, or you live in a plush apartment with lots of amenities. In the short term, you are correct in thinking that renting in areas where property values are falling is smart. After all, all you have to do is make the monthly rent. You get to live in a nice place and not lose money.

But in the long term, you do lose. *Rental apartments with lots of amenities are velvet prisons; your monthly rent is destined to make others rich, not you.* You are putting lifestyle ahead of long-term wealth-building.

Just know that for most people, owning their first residence has proven to be their best investment. And your first home will not be your dream home.

Since lack of saving for a down payment is the barrier that stops most first-time homebuyers, I have included two websites that source government grants to **help you buy your first residence:**

1. www.hud.gov/local/local/ca/buying/prgrmscity.com Registry for all government grant programs (www.hud.gov/local/ca/buying/prgm-scity.cf)

2. www.ncsha.org National Council of State Housing Agencies (Find the government agency in your state that will provide financial assistance or maybe even a free down payment for your first home.)

CHAPTER 13

Flipping REOs
for Fun and Profit

Buying and selling REOs requires intimate knowledge of the market place. Once you have found an REO that looks like a good deal, it is very important for you to know how to calculate the amount of potential profit you can make before you purchase the property. In this chapter you will learn an easy formula to calculate the amount of potential profit a property has in it.

Before you learn this formula, it is important to remember that you want to purchase flipper properties for no more than 65% of their market value. This gives you a 35% discount. If the property needs more than cosmetic repairs such as painting and carpeting, deduct the cost of the other repairs from your offer. You need a 35% margin because of the many costs involved with each deal—if you offer more, you do so at your own peril.

To figure the potential profit in a deal, there are different costs that must be considered beforehand. Here is a detailed explanation of each cost:

1. Purchase price
2. Settlement cost: Settlement costs are all the costs associated with the buying and selling of a property. When a property settlement occurs, both the buyer and the seller of the property have costs that must be paid in order for the ownership of the property to change. These costs are for loan fees, attorney's fees, title charges,

transfer taxes, fees charged to record the new deed, etc. Use 2% - 3% of the purchase price as a general estimate of the amount you will pay for the purchaser's side of the settlement costs.

3. Fix-up costs: These are all the costs associated with getting the REO into top marketing condition so that it will show well and sell quickly. Examples of fix-up costs are painting and carpeting; plumbing and electrical repairs; renovation or updating of kitchens and bathrooms, if needed; and any other repairs you must do to get the property into sellable condition.

4. Carrying costs: These are your monthly costs such as monthly loan payments, property taxes, monthly utility bills, and monthly hazard insurance premiums. Most lenders require more expensive builders' or contractors' insurance You should factor in at least four months of carrying costs.

    a. Loan payments and taxes will be about 1% of the amount you are borrowing.

    b. Consider utilities and insurance, such as electricity, gas and water, and hazard insurance.

5. Marketing costs: These are the total costs for marketing your property and going to settlement on it once your agent finds a buyer. Use 12% as a general estimate:

    a. Six percent for your real estate agent's commission and 6% for the seller's settlement fees. Buyers will need all the help they can get in today's challenging lending environment and economy.

    (Now this may sound ridiculous but, trust me, it is not. Many buyers have barely enough money for their down payment and cannot afford to buy the home from you unless you help them with their settlement fees. Because many buyers will ask you to help pay their settlement costs, you will need to be prepared for it. Part of being prepared is remembering to factor this cost into the formula and calculating your potential profit before you purchase a property.)

6. Profit: How much is your time worth?

You now know the six big costs you must add together in order to find the amount of potential profit you will make. Because fix-up costs vary with each property, there is no percentage that can be used for that in the formula. You will need to get a contractor to give you estimates on your first few deals. Once you have completed a few deals, you will be able to start estimating fix-up costs on your own.

Why Flip?

Flip as a means to buy houses to keep. After writing over 100 pages extolling the virtues of buy-and-hold investing, here I am, advising how to flip. Absolutely.

To get the money for down payments, many investors will flip a few, keep a few and so on. I know some of the best professional property flippers in California, and they are in the enviable position of keeping their best property and selling the lesser ones. Which properties do they keep?

1. Single-family houses (three-bedroom/two-bathroom)
2. Class 'A' neighborhoods
3. Properties close to home, easier to manage
4. Higher-end areas
5. Best cash flows
6. To eventually sell and retire debt on other keepers

Selling Strategies

This blossoming REO market will afford opportunities for flippers who employ innovative financing techniques. With the lack of liquidity in the market (banks are not so investor-friendly these days), to make any money you may have to be the bank.

Unlike the banks that are in trouble today, you don't want to buy beyond your limits to lend. But tremendous opportunities are to be had if you are offering ways for borrowers to buy your house when the banks are not.

To discuss this in detail would require a separate seminar, but I urge you to learn more about these six creative ways to sell for income or cash:

1. Creating notes
   a. Wraparound mortgages
   b. Create the note, sell it at a discount for cash
   c. Assign the note, sell it to cash investor
2. Wholesale house to investors
3. Installment sale
4. Lease options

5. Assign purchase contract for cash
6. Buy houses, sell some to pay off your keepers
7. Sell houses that need fixing to handymen

If you buy REO flippers at substantial discounts, you are in the driver's seat.

Your skill at buying discounted REOs and selling them on terms will benefit: passive cash investors, cash-strapped first-timers, IRA and Roth IRA holders, your kids wanting to get their start, and many others who don't have your skill at working with banks.

CHAPTER 14

It Will Get Better

If you are immersed in a declining market in which values are falling like a rock, houses appear to not sell for any price, out-migrates are leaving the state in droves and neighborhoods with boarded-up houses proliferate, it may seem like economic Armageddon is striking once again.

Let's keep things in perspective by examining again what a market bottom looks like:

1. Monthly sales volume is increasing (moving average showing strong upward trend)
2. More first-time homebuyers entering the market
3. Still a lot of naysayers predicting prices will go down further
4. Recovery is "patchy"—not all areas recovering at the same time
5. Monthly foreclosure rate declining
6. Sideways price trend—"choppy" and hard-to-discern direction
7. Listings decrease
8. More in-migration from out of state
9. Most people have given up on real estate
10. Builder concessions and "giveaways" disappear
11. Builders start pulling more permits than in previous months

Buy when things are at their darkest and when there is blood in the streets. Buy at the sound of canons, sell at the sound of trumpets.

Real Estate Investing Works in All Markets
Strategies of investing in a changing market:

- Stage 1: The Bottom
- Stage 2: The Beginning
- Stage 3: Nearing the Peak
- Stage 4: The Early Decline
- Stage 5: The Steep Decline

Stage 1: The Bottom
At the bottom, cash is king. The key is to have liquidity when nobody else has any. Many investors make long-term investments mostly with their own cash during this time since it is hard to find any joint ventures or equity shares. By the time you hit this point, after years of protracted declines and heavy foreclosure volumes with builders and mortgage companies closing shop, it is hard to find other investors who think in a contrary fashion.

Deep discounts are to be had by buying properties in peripheral areas with cash. Hold onto those distant properties until business expansion heads your way. Condos in bulk can be bought very cheaply in multi-unit purchases from the banks.

Try to have little debt service because it is hard to know how long before liquidity will return to the market. Being able to hold onto lots, land, houses and apartments for at least five years without big debt service is wise because there will be no rapid appreciation for at least that long.

You can be very aggressive about buying properties in outlying areas for pennies on the dollar. Many investors buy fully entitled lots from builders or their foreclosing lenders for less than the costs of improvements. The builders have put hard money into permits, roads and utilities at their cost; you get the land thrown in for free.

Neighborhoods will look more beat up as speculators give their houses back to the banks. Formerly owner-occupied areas become rental neighborhoods until price appreciation returns. For now, many marginal neighborhoods will suffer from "disinvestment," when money is leaving the neighborhood.

Many successful, long-term real estate business owners started their operations during these times; most have prospered as the systems they have put into place pay off when the market heats up.

Contractors can buy deeply discounted detached homes, fix them up and add square footage, creating equity that adds to profit margins. As always, being well-located in a high-demand area means your property will sell quickly.

Realtors allied with banks should focus their marketing efforts to the first-time homebuyer, as affordability is at its strongest here.

REO volumes will start to lessen toward the end of this cycle as the inventory starts to clean out. Banks discount less on price as their balance sheets become less bloated with repossessed property.

Invest in financial stocks or homebuilding stocks by finding companies that have weathered the downturn. If management is smart enough to still be around after a protracted downturn, they have good long-term prospects in an up-trending market.

Stage 2: The Beginning

At the beginning of the up cycle, make sure you buy with long-term financing. Keep an eye out for the next cities that will become great locations as the market expands.

Be very aggressive in buying houses, land and apartments since your downside is limited. Banks will slowly start lending money again so be aware of any new loan programs as they come online. Banks will still be gun-shy. It is time to start pulling your cash out of properties with equity to invest in better areas and in better properties.

Real estate business operators should start investing (slowly) in their businesses, hiring staff and improving efficiencies. Consider branding your firm so it is not personality-driven to prepare for a future sale to a bigger firm.

Creative investors buying properties have the best of both worlds here: Sellers are still distressed form the previous cycle but have increasing equity. Bank loans are still scarce.

The bank's repossessed inventory is starting to thin, and deep discounts become rare, except for boondock properties, condos, condo conversions and turn-of-the-century houses or serious fixers.

Landlords will see their rents soften as renters rush to buy starter homes.

Stage 3: Nearing the Peak

For long-term buy-and-hold investors, this is the best time to retire debt. Sell your worst properties (condos, out of area or older fixers) in order to pay off your well-located properties that rent quickly. Rents are likely to increase well as fewer buyers can buy and will need to rent properties close to work centers and highways/mass transit areas. *Foreclosures will push people back into the rental markets.*

Creative investors working directly with distressed sellers can find properties priced well below market since the banks have no REO inventory.

Real estate business owners should consider selling their companies because growth-oriented firms tend to overpay for established companies during this part of the cycle. You might also want to pay yourself a lot of money by going public, although you will certainly create a lot of expenses and headaches if you choose that route. Put even more money into process efficiency in all of your endeavors: buy/sell real estate, lending, building/developing, or being a landlord. In hot markets it is easy to become sloppy, overpay for properties and not keep your rents to market. Scrutinize every deal more carefully with an eye to the coming downturn.

Avoid downside risk by using joint ventures or equity shares. JV capital will be plentiful. At this stage, the risk is highest and so is the short-term return. In this last cycle, "Stage 3: Nearing the Peak" lasted for years. You never know for sure when the end of an expansion will occur; you only know the market top once you have passed it.

Builders should implement an "asset light" strategy in which you only own the land you need to fund operations, but have plenty of options with well-capitalized land developers and partners so you won't run out of land during a downturn. Concentrate on locations where there are fewer homebuilders. Shed any high-density attached projects (apartments, condos or condo conversions) because the builder demand will be high today, but the consumer demand will be low tomorrow.

Stage 4: The Early Decline

A flood of unrealistically priced listings comes after the market tops out. Astute buyers ignore them. Sellers must be aggressive early and not chase the market down. Look for buyers with large amounts of cash down as loan programs start going away. Foreclosures will start flooding the market very soon.

Sales in outlying areas soften; stay away from them because soon they will become very volatile. Landlords will soon find these houses harder to rent the farther they are from work centers.

Sell your financial stocks before they dip and sell your junkier houses at a discount. Dump over-leveraged property even if you have to write a check. Better to take your lumps earlier than later.

Start building cash reserves now. Look to lock in all your keeper property with long-term debt. Stay away from taking cash out unless you can afford the debt service. Establish lines of credit with high limits, but do not use them until we near the bottom. The exception to this rule is if you can buy a deeply discounted property and quickly turn it by pricing it way below market.

Developers should sell their land to the eternal optimists at a perceived discount. Cultivate your banking relationships, as those people will be the land sellers of the future. *Banks will start repossessing property shortly so REO buyers should establish relationships with established bank brokers. Banks rehire brokers they have used in the past but will soon need new ones.*

Real estate providers should orient their operations towards the marketing and selling of bank property, since they will soon have all the listings. Boondock property, condo conversions and condos show up on their lists first. Investors should resist the urge to buy them as they will become much cheaper.

Soon, Realtors doing BPOs and short sales, appraisers doing drive-bys and walk-throughs, and lender workout departments will all be very busy.

If you wish to sell your business and it has not sold, hire a very good business broker and pay him well to aggressively market it because the window is closing.

Pay down or refinance your short-term debt obligations into long-term debt and build up cash reserves by selling your homes and land as quickly as possible, even at a loss. The loss will be greater later. Many believe that losing money is somehow a sign of failure and is disastrous to the balance sheet. They are wrong. This is a cyclical business. Recovering as much of the cash that you have already spent is what matters. Hire a great tax advisor, too.

The downturns are always longer and more painful than people think they will be. Raise some money for the future, but don't spend it.

Stage 5: The Steep Decline

All of your preparation should have paid off. While this isn't fun for you, it is worse for others. Pay off all of the debt you are obligated to pay. Survival mode begins here. Properties bought for cash will be deeply discounted.

Banks' repossessed inventory will start to bloat. REO properties will be the leading edge of price declines in formerly hot areas. Banks are notoriously inefficient in disposing of their inventory. Exploit those inefficiencies. Many properties are left unfinished by foreclosed homeowners in the middle of a rehab. Contractors can get an additional 10% to 20% price discount by buying from banks.

Consider starting a "vulture fund" with investors since banks will sell off their troubled properties in multi-million-dollar blocks for fifty to sixty cents on the dollar. Try to take the cream properties in 'AA' neighborhoods for long-term holds while wholesaling the 'B' and 'C' grade properties to investors or retail buyers.

Homebuilders should build homes for troubled banks or finish the ones left unfinished, and find equity partners in a structure that provides them most of the upside and, more importantly, protects them from any downside. If you have too much debt, take your lumps. Your credit report will not be the only one marked up with late pays or foreclosures. Before that happens, work with the lenders to help them short sell your upside down properties. If that does not happen, try to qualify for a loan modification if you wish to keep the property. A deed-in-lieu-of-foreclosure is better than a foreclosure on your credit report.

With the lender, negotiate the debt to be non-recourse. Recent tax laws enable short sale sellers to avoid loan forgiveness being taxed as 1099 income—a BIG bonus and another incentive to work with the lenders.

Conclusion

Many of the smartest companies in our business, run by veterans of several housing cycles, have implemented many of the strategies above. The majority of the smaller and younger companies in our business have not. All builders, however, wish they had done more off-balance-sheet or option agreements and sold more land. Every investor wishes he had sold more houses.

This year and at least part of next year are going to prove to be very difficult, but you will learn more than you have ever learned and you will emerge a smarter and better company (or perhaps even a new company) or buyer. The demand for housing will continue to trend upward for the rest of your life, but there will be significant bumps along the way. Managing through the bumps is the challenge, and those who do it deserve the greatest recognitions and rewards.

CHAPTER 15

Demographics Are Destiny

Cities worldwide have been the economic growth engines and will be in the future. In 1800, just 3% of the world's population lived in cities, according to the United Nations. Now, more than 50% of our planet's 5.5 billion people are city dwellers. Cities are nothing more than a collection of neighborhoods, and if the neighborhood where you invest is located near or at the edge of major metro job centers, you have a stable and intact demand for housing.

Whenever I buy a house, I look at the neighborhood. I ask myself, "Why is the neighborhood important, and why do I want to let my money ride in it?" As my mentor, Dr. Schumacher, so aptly puts it, "Value is nothing more than the contemplation of future benefits."

Demand for single-family houses in pride-of-ownership neighborhoods comes from factors not so readily apparent:

1. Overall economic trends: job growth, personal incomes
2. Quality, convenience and availability of facilities: cultural centers, schools, churches, parks, shopping and public transportation
3. Land and improvement characteristics: street patterns and nearby commercial structures, good or bad
4. Harmony of development
5. Pride of ownership: trees and roads

6. Real estate sales activity
7. Number of foreclosures

I would remind you that my home county of Orange County, CA, was once no more than orange groves and soybean fields, an agricultural neighbor to the commercial behemoth that is Los Angeles. Primarily a commuter community that had an amusement park (Disneyland), Orange County's economy was reliant on defense work fed by the Vietnam War and the Cold War. By the 1990s, hundreds of thousands of aeronautical workers and engineers were laid off, leaving behind a highly educated workforce intent on staying in the state.

Because of this highly educated workforce, start-up companies in the high-tech, bio-tech and nano-tech industries surged, and now Southern California is drawing venture capital at a faster rate than San Francisco or New England, the two other top attractions for venture capital funding in the U.S. Southern California's VC investments grew 23% in the first quarter last year from the same quarter in 2006, while the Bay Area's grew 10% and New England's declined. Most of the area's money was for Internet technology (IT) research.

From 1998 to 2006, Orange County's median house price almost tripled. Over the next half-century, California's population will explode by nearly 75%, and Riverside will surpass its bigger neighbors to become the second most populous county after Los Angeles, according to the state's Department of Finance.

Population Increases

COUNTY	2000	2050	%
	in millions		
Riverside	1.6	4.7	203
Imperial	.14	.39	170
San Bern.	1.7	3.7	113
Ventura	.76	1.2	62
San Diego	2.8	4.5	59
Orange	2.9	4.0	39
Los Angeles	9.6	13.1	36
CALIFORNIA	34.1	59.5	74

California As a World Economy

California's population will surpass that of the entire country of Italy by 2040, but the United States will probably not be the largest economy in the world if China's growth rate of 8%-10% is sustained. Here are the largest economies in the world, ranked by GDP:

1. United States
2. Japan
3. Germany

4. Mainland China
5. United Kingdom
6. France
7. Italy
8. **California**

By 2040, the biggest world economies in order of GDP are projected to be:

1. China
2. United States
3. India
4. **California**

California will near the 60 million mark in 2050. According to the Department of Finance, California's population will rise from 34.1 million in 2000 to 59.5 million at the mid-century point. And *its projected growth rate in those fifty years will outstrip the national rate—nearly 75% compared with less than 50%* projected by the federal government. That could translate into increased political clout in Washington, D.C.

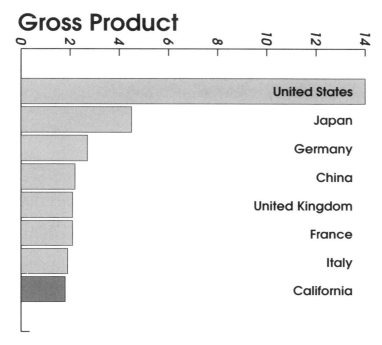

Southern California's population is projected to grow at a rate of more than 60%, according to the new state figures, reaching 31.6 million by mid-century. That's an increase of 12.1 million over just seven counties. The numbers underscore most demographers' view that the *state's population is pushing east, from both Los Angeles and the Bay Area to counties such as Riverside and San Bernardino as well as half a dozen or so smaller Central Valley counties.*

L.A. County alone will top 13 million by 2050, an increase of almost 3.5 million residents. And Riverside County—long among the fastest-growing in the state—will triple in population to 4.7 million by mid-century.

Riverside County will add 3.1 million people, according to the new state figures, eclipsing Orange and San Diego to become the second most populous in the state. With less expensive housing than the coast, Riverside County has grown by more than 472,000 residents since 2000, according to state estimates.

Growth will be most dramatic beyond the city of Riverside as the patches of empty space around communities such as Palm Springs, Perris and Hemet begin to fill in with housing tracts. The Coachella Valley, for example, will become fully developed and seem like less of a distinct area outside of Riverside.

Expect a lot of the new development in Riverside County to go up along the 215 Freeway between Perris and Murrieta. Thousands of homes have popped up in that area in the last decade, and Goldman said applications for that area indicate that condominiums are next. The department is so busy that he's hiring ten people who'll start in the next months.

Sutter County, for example, is expected to be the fastest-growing on a percentage basis between 2000 and 2050, jumping 255% to a population of 282,894, according to the state. Kern County is expected to see its population more than triple to 2.1 million by mid-century.

In Southern California, San Diego County is projected to grow by almost 1.7 million residents and Orange County by 1.1 million. Even Ventura County—where voters have imposed some limits on urban sprawl—will see its population jump 62% to more than 1.2 million, if the projections hold.

Figures show that the majority of California's growth will be in the Latino population, according to Dowell Myers, a professor of urban planning and demography at USC. He added that "68% of the growth this decade will be Latino,

75% next and 80% after that." Though the state's growth is young and Latino, the majority of voters will be older and white—at least for the next decade.

But Aren't People Moving out of California?

Los Angeles had a domestic population outflow of 6% in six years since 2000—balanced by an immigrant inflow of 6%. The numbers are the same for these eight metro areas as a whole.

Census Bureau data tells us that more people move to California every year, except in 1994-1998 and now. Last year, the state had 128,000 more people moving in than moving out.

Moving vans being rented tell us where people are moving. You want to invest in areas that are high-growth and economically dynamic. Allied Van Lines' moving data for 2007 shows that 52% of its California moves were outbound, down from last year's 57%.

Five percent fewer people are leaving the state. Excellent! That is very good news for California because property investors there will have an abundant supply of renters.

Competitor United Van Lines showed 50.8% of its California moves were outbound in 2007, the lowest rate in five years. Van moves are usually seen as a barometer of management-level relocations. This reinforces the notion that not as many families find California tough to call home, due to declining housing costs.

It's a great trend! More people are moving back to California and the stage is being set for the next boom.

Along the coasts (New York, Los Angeles, San Francisco, San Diego, Chicago—on the coast of Lake Michigan, Miami, Washington and Boston, there is a pattern you don't find in other big cities. Americans are moving out and immigrants are moving in, in very large numbers, with low overall population growth for the past six years.

This is something few would have predicted twenty years ago. Americans are now moving out of, not into, coastal California, and in very large numbers they're moving out of our largest metro areas.

The domestic outflow from these metro areas is 3.9 million people, 650,000 a year, due to:

- High housing costs
- High taxes
- Distaste, in some cases, for the burgeoning immigrant populations—this is driving many Americans elsewhere

The result is that these coastal megalopolises are an increasingly two-tiered society: large affluent populations happily contemplating (at least until recently) their rapidly rising housing values and large, mostly immigrant, working classes laboring at low wages and struggling to move up the economic ladder. The economic divide in New York and Los Angeles is starting to look like the economic divide in Mexico City and São Paulo.

What About the Rest of the Country?

In 1950, the population of the U.S. was 150 million. Today, the latest census estimate for the nation is 301 million, more than twice as many people. People in America move around. We will be 400 million strong by 2040 and 600 million strong by 2060.

The top ten cities a hundred years ago would have included places like Baltimore (now at 631,366, the nineteenth largest), Boston (590,763, twenty-second), Cleveland (444,313, fortieth) and St. Louis (347,181, fifty-second).

Los Angeles, the nation's second largest city with 3,849,378 people, had a population of just over 100,000 in 1900. Dallas, Houston, San Antonio, San Diego and San Jose, CA, all had fewer than 100,000.

Phoenix, which a hundred years ago was not even among the one hundred most populous cities, grew by more than 40,000 residents during the twelve months that ended July 1, 2006. It passed Philadelphia, which has lost about 70,000 residents during the 2000s, to become the fifth biggest American city.

Interior Boomtowns

Each of the ten biggest cities once lay within five hundred miles of the Canadian border. Now, seven of the top ten are Sun Belt cities, closer to Chihuahua than Toronto.

Some of the nation's biggest cities today were mere blips on the radar at the turn of twentieth-century America. Population has flowed from the Snow Belt to the Sun Belt, from an industrially ailing East and Midwest to an economically vibrant West and South. But the actual picture of recent growth, as measured by the 2000 census and the census estimates for 2006, is more complicated.

Interior boomtowns (none of which touch the Atlantic or Pacific coasts) have had population growths of 18% in six years. They've had considerable immigrant inflow of 4%, but with the exceptions of Dallas and Houston, this immigrant inflow has been dwarfed by a much larger domestic inflow—3 million to 1.5 million overall. Domestic inflow has been a whopping:

1. Nineteen percent in Las Vegas
2. Fifteen percent in the Inland Empire (California's Riverside and San Bernardino Counties, where much of the outflow from Los Angeles has gone)
3. Thirteen percent in Orlando and Charlotte
4. Twelve percent in Phoenix
5. Ten percent in Tampa
6. Nine percent in Jacksonville

Domestic inflow was over 200,000 in the *Inland Empire, Phoenix, Atlanta, Las Vegas and Orlando.* These are economic dynamos that are driving much of America's growth.

There is less economic polarization there than in the coastal megalopolises.

•   Dallas is now larger than San Francisco.
•   Houston is now larger than Detroit.
•   Atlanta is now larger than Boston.
•   Charlotte is now larger than Milwaukee.
•   San Antonio has more domestic than immigrant inflow even though the border is only a three-hour drive away.

The interior boomtowns generated 38% of the nation's population growth in 2000-2006, as opposed to the coastal cities. This can be ascribed to:

•   Problems with families in an urbanized setting
•   Kids not able to walk anywhere because of the traffic
•   People not knowing each other
•   Parents not being able to stay home with their kids or continuing to send them to public schools
•   In interior boomtowns, people can actually afford a beautiful house in a nice neighborhood.

The highest-growing counties since 2000 have been:

•   McKinney, Texas, which lies in the path of the outward expansion of Dallas. This is the fastest growing of any city with more than a 50,000 population. It has nearly doubled in size since 2000 to 107,530.

- Gilbert, Arizona (increased 73.9% to 191,517)
- Northern Las Vegas (increased 71.1% to 197,567)
- Port St. Lucie, Florida (increased 61.9% to 143,868)

Since demographics and moving patterns are so vital, they can help you answer perhaps the most important question in real estate, which we will examine in the next chapter.

CHAPTER 16

What Will My Property Be Worth Five, Ten and Twenty Years From Now?

The short answer is, "More." How much more has to do with where you buy. If positive conditions now exist where you want to be, will those reasons to invest still be there five, ten or twenty years in the future?

Remember me telling you about how Orange County, CA, used to be a commuter community for Los Angeles? Let me tell you a story told to me by a man who worked at a Douglas Aircraft assembly plant in Long Beach, CA, just north of Orange County.

"At lunchtime at the plant, we had all sorts of people giving lectures and pitching products. One time, we even had Ronald Reagan come and talk to us about the Cold War.

One day, we had these builders come and tell us about this new housing project twenty miles to the south of the plant where we could buy a house for $29,000. They said there was no shopping and the houses had nothing around them but orange orchards. I remember thinking to myself, *Why would I drive all the way down there and spend that kind of money for a house in the middle of nowhere when I can buy a nice house in Long Beach for half that?*"

He went on to say, "I wish I had bought a boatload of those houses in Mission Viejo, California, because they are all worth about $750,000 each now."

Look at the Past to See Your Future

Is this elevated pace of price inflation likely to continue? The growth you see in the charts shows that, from 2000-2005, the trend of houses in California appreciating by double digits became unsustainable. Now we see appreciation rates approaching negative numbers. In the years 1992-1996, the Western region had negative appreciation of 1%-4%, indicating that house prices scraped along the bottom for over four years.

Between 2003 and 2005, most regions of the U.S. showed hyper-appreciation, particularly the West. These last few years of appreciation should not have happened, but they did due to the unprecedented confluence of three factors:

1.   The savings and loan bailout of the 1980s started a new era of loan securitization;
2.   The 1998 Asian crisis fed a global savings glut;
3.   The tech bust of the late 1990s ushered in low interest rates.

The Wall Street securitization of conventional mortgages had its genesis in the early 1990s when the federal Resolution Trust Corporation took over savings and loans that held more than $400 billion of assets. Though some thought it would take the RTC a century to unload them, it took only a few years. The agency successfully securitized new classes of assets, ushering in a new era of Wall Street's appetite for loans backed by American real estate.

Thailand had devalued its currency in 1997, touching off a crisis in the region that led other countries to devalue and in some cases default on foreign debt. China was going to devalue their currency, but did not because the U.S. did not want anther round of currency devaluations as the Japanese yen was sliding. The U.S. urged the Chinese to hold their peg, and praised them when they did so.

Determined never to be so tied to the onerous conditions of the International Monetary Fund, these countries have kept those policies in place. Thai reserves, effectively exhausted in 1997, now stand at $73 billion.

With the tech bust of the 1990s, the Fed cut interest rates to the lowest level in a generation to avoid a severe downturn. But even by mid-2003, job creation and business investment were still anemic, and the inflation rate was slipping toward 1%. The Fed began to study Japan's unhappy bout with deflation (generally declining prices), which made it harder to repay debts and left the central bank seemingly powerless to stimulate growth.

With the prime rate held at such a low rate, mortgage money became

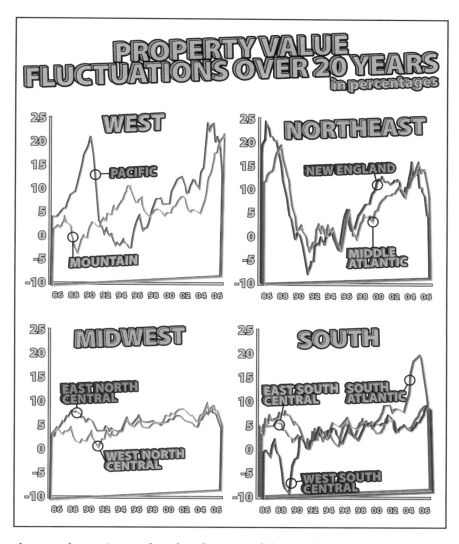

cheap and easy. It was abundant because of the worldwide savings glut and since Wall Street created sophisticated securities that added lots of cash to the market, real estate investors and marginal homebuyers took notice and borrowed to excess. The seeds of this current housing slowdown were sown almost twenty years ago.

And now we see the demise of an entire class of mortgages that fed the boom. The main lenders that provided ALT-A credit are up in smoke, or are severely hobbled. Buyers are scared, easy mortgage money is gone and interest rates are not going down any time soon.

The Road Ahead

The bottom of the housing market is likely to last longer than most people think. This protracted REO market will provide opportunity for astute real estate investors who have cash, or the means to get it. When you can buy well-located houses in high-demand neighborhoods for a fraction of what they were worth, this reduces the biggest risk in all of real estate.

As the foreign money that had filled up the credit derivative structures that Wall Street created is now drying up, finding bank loans will remain a

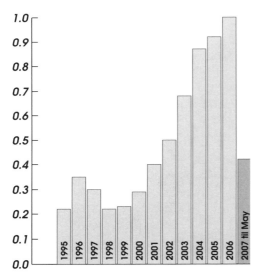

challenge even as beleaguered Fannie Mae and Freddie Mac will seek to push more money into the market and up their loan limits for the more expensive coastal areas (likewise for the Federal Home Administration). Liquidity will return to the real estate markets, but it will take time before Wall Street's appetite for mortgage-backed securities comes back.

Ten years from now, you will look back and wonder at the opportunities you missed if you don't take advantage of this lender-distressed market now.

Although the money that fueled this real estate boom and went into these credit derivatives has dissipated, the ability to create this financing system remains and will re-emerge in a different form. The structure is in place for new money to fund fully documented loans with lower LTVs and higher credit scores.

Distressed property for sale by the banks will be the story that closes this first decade of the twenty-first century. An opportunity like this will most likely not present itself again for another real estate cycle—at least ten years. The question is: How will you write your own story?

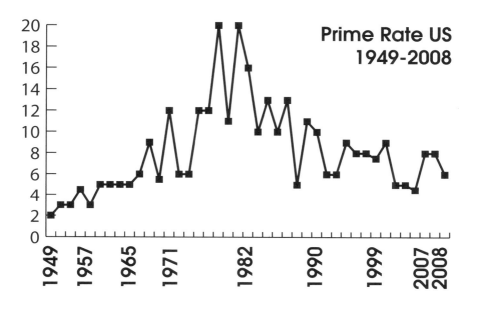

GOOD LUCK AND HAPPY HUNTING!

*"The prices of houses seem to have reached a plateau,
and there is reasonable expectancy that prices will decline."*
—**Time Magazine, 1947**

*"Houses cost too much for the mass market. Today's average price is around
$8,000 — out of the reach for two-thirds of all buyers."*
—**Science Digest, 1948**

*"The goal of owning a home seems to be getting beyond the reach of more and
more Americans. The typical new house today costs about $28,000."*
—**Business Week, 1969**

*"You might well be suspicious of 'common wisdom'
that tells you, 'Don't wait, buy now...continuing inflation
will force home prices and rents higher and higher."*
—**NEA Journal, 1970**

*"The median price of a home today is approaching $50,000...
Housing experts predict price rises in the future won't be that great."*
—**Nations Business, 1977**

*"The era of easy profits in real estate may be
drawing to a close."*
—**Money Magazine, 1981**

"The golden-age of risk-free run-ups in home prices is gone."
—**Money Magazine, 1985**

*"Most economists agree...[a home] will become little more
than a roof and a tax deduction, certainly not the lucrative
investment it was through much of the 1980s."*
—**Money Magazine, 1986**

*"Financial planners agree that houses will
continue to be a poor investment."*
—**Kiplinger's Personal Financial Magazine, 1993**

"A home is where the bad investment is."
—**San Francisco Examiner, 1996**

*What You Owe Today Is
What You Will Be Worth Tomorrow*

REAL ESTATE
DEBT CAN MAKE
YOU RICH

▶ The right kind of loan for every situation

▶ Covers 100 percent financing,
no-money-down, and seller financing

▶ Insider advice on the tax benefits of
real estate debt

STEVE DEXTER

Steve Dexter, a frequent contributor to CNN/Money, Fox TV and CBS Radio, is also a distinguished speaker at Harvard Business School, Harvard Law School and the Graduate School of Design. A real estate consultant since 1990, Steve is the author of *Real Estate Debt Can Make You Rich*, published by McGraw-Hill, which was rated as one of the top five real estate books by Washington Post Media. Steve teaches courses in investing and real estate finance at colleges across Southern California.